Vibrancy Publishing

Vibrancy Ins., LLC

Cover design and editorial design by Daniela Esponda Rodíguez
Nature Design Lab.
Index by Amber Purcell

Agreements: Your Choice / by James L. Ritchie-Dunham

ISBN# 978-0-9907153-2-0 (pbk.)
1. Agreements. 2. Big Yes!. 3. Your Choice. 4. Title.

First edition 2024

9 8 7 6 5 4 3 2 1

With gratitude to the four generations I live with now.
My parents.
My brothers and wife.
My kids.
My first grandchild.
For those who choose to say Yes! every day in every way.

AGREEMENTS

Your Choice

by

James L. Ritchie-Dunham

ACKNOWLEDGEMENTS

I am grateful to the many teachers who have continuously shown up in my life. Friends, acquaintances, business partners, clients, students, fellow researchers and teachers. Unexpected events, deepening relationships, persistent patterns. Inspired observers from the past, those seeing the world afresh today, and those pointing ways forward. They all help me refine, every day, my agreements. My Yes!

For this book you are holding, I am specifically grateful to Maureen Metcalf for reading the first draft and providing reflections from years of writing and publishing her own amazing books, and to Jay Harris, who you will meet later in the book, for his careful reading of the manuscript.

I am always grateful to my wife, who for 33 years has provided the on-going context for my agreements, as well as specific thoughts and process around getting this book into publishing form. A Big YES! to my Leslie.

Initial Conditions

Whether you have a great day, an okay day, or a bad day, it all depends on how you started. We found through our years of research at leading universities, and our work all over the world with real teams and organizations, families, and communities, as well as networks, that the initial conditions you start with determine the experience that you have and the outcomes you achieve. How you see the world, how you engage it, and the agreements that you have about it. That's it.

The great day that you had, of being seen and appreciated. You learned about yourself, growing, seeing the best contributions that you and others can make. You got feedback from the world of the impact you were having. All of that, in its creativity, is an expression, in a great day, of some initial conditions that said Yes! to the world.

Your other experience, of a mediocre day, where you learned something. Your skill sets were appreciated. You saw some of the skills and things that others could do. They brought them to the game, somewhat. You cooperated with them and your team did okay. There was some learning and appreciation of some of that creativity. The expression of that creativity led to some good outcomes and some decent experiences.

Or you had an awful day. Nobody even saw you for what you were bringing today. You didn't learn anything. You were exhausted from not being able to show up and do anything. Nobody saw or appreciated you. You didn't really even notice what others were doing. Anybody could replace you in what you were doing. You were focused on just doing the job and getting it done. The outcomes and experiences reflected that.

The understanding is that these are agreements that you have, about what is real, how you engage in the world, how you see others, the different resources you access, how you make decisions, how you enforce decisions, the criteria you use, what you value, how you interact. Those are all agreements. These agreements influence your interactions. How you see the world influences your agreements. How you see the world influences your agreements, which influence how you interact with others, and that influences the experience you have and the outcomes you achieve.

The agreements you have in any given situation, whether with your family at breakfast, your friends for a coffee, or in a meeting at work, all start with an underlying way of looking at the world. A set of assumptions about how the world works. These are your initial conditions in that situation and these initial conditions determine the unspoken agreements that will guide your interactions. This will determine the experience you have and the outcomes you achieve. It all starts with the initial conditions.

What can you do about this? To improve your situation, to have more of your experiences be the ones that are pretty good or great, then what you can start to do is to make explicit, to be able to see, what those agreements are. Which agreements am I experiencing? Which would I choose? How do I choose them? How do I choose them with you? What are the initial conditions that determine these agreements? What could be the initial conditions? How do we see how the initial conditions determine the agreements that impact the experience we have and the outcomes that we achieve, so that we can adjust them, together, over time?

You can try this by looking at what are some of the basic agreements that you have? Are you having the experience that you know is available to you in this group or with someone else? Are you both having the experience you want? That can be the first step, saying, "You know what? I don't agree with this experience. I think we're capable of doing better. Not like other people, but us. How we're doing. What we could be doing. Do you agree with me? Do you see that we could be doing better?" Then you can start to look at it. As you go through the chapters of this book, you will see what initial conditions you start with, what agreements you have and how to go about shifting them.

NET POSITIVE VS NET NEGATIVE

These initial conditions are as simple as starting with a Yes! or a No! If you start with a No!, you end up in net negative. If you start with a Yes!, you end up in net positive. It's that simple, and shocking.

Net positive means that the benefits of what you're doing, the upside, the positive, is greater than the cost of what you're doing or the negative side, what you're not taking advantage of, what you are losing. Net negative means that the cost of what you're doing is greater than the benefit. You end up losing. Net net, you are worse off, in the negative. And net net in the positive, you are better off.

If you start with a No! in your initial conditions, you will end up with a net negative. A net negative experience and outcome. If you start with a Yes!, you will end up with a net positive. A net positive experience and outcome. Always.

We have found no examples of groups that start with a No! that end up net positive. All groups that start with a No! end up with net negative. Even the really good ones. Likewise, everyone that starts with a Yes!, always end up net positive. Even the worst functioning of the groups that start with a Yes! always end up net positive.

The framing is simple. If you start with No!, you're going to end up losing more than you gain. If you start with Yes!, you're going to end up gaining more than you lose.

In the example of the group that was not very good, you experienced not being seen, not appreciated, being replaceable, looking for the one, already-given way to do things, focusing only on the outcomes. This is starting with the initial condition of No! In that group, the cost of losing all the contributions that you could have made, of being disengaged, of not making your contribution is far greater than the positive impact of the little work that you did, and the little creativity that did come through. In the group where you had a great experience, the benefits of being seen and appreciated, in contributing your best with others, all that synergy and learning, in evolution, is far greater than any cost for having you in the group.

What we have found, through our research, documenting the evidence basis of this finding, is that when you start with a No!, the best you can achieve is still net negative. If you start with a Yes!, then the least you'll get is still net positive. The initial conditions lead to net positive or net negative. This is a choice. The outcomes, the experiences are clear, either net negative or net positive.

YES! TO LIFE AND LOVE OR NO!

In these initial conditions, what are you saying Yes! to? Or No! to? You are saying Yes! to life. To love. What does this look like? When you are saying Yes!, you are saying Yes! to you, to your life, to your expression, to your creative contribution. To what it is yours to do.

Saying Yes! to another, and what is theirs to contribute. What they are here to do. What is their learning, their potential, their creative output.

Saying Yes! to us. What we bring. What we are learning, along the way. What we care about. What we each uniquely contribute, so that we can achieve something far greater together than by ourselves.

Saying Yes! to creative processes. To seeing possibilities, to learning and trying things out, to getting the outcomes, to getting the feedback, and then to learning from all of that and adjusting.

Saying Yes! to the creativity that is ours, everywhere. To this purposeful energy that is everywhere. For us to say Yes! to. It's saying Yes! to abundance. To seeing an abundant life. To seeing that all of this is possible—it is just a matter of us saying Yes!

What is No!? No is saying No! to your own creativity. It is not really a true thing. Not really here. Not now. It's just your current capacity to do something, if even that. No learning. No potential. Not here. You do not trust the environment enough to do that. You do not trust the other enough to do that. You do not trust the group enough to do that. It's saying No! to the other. No! to the other's learning or creativity. You did not ask what the other could do. It is just what they are bringing right now, maybe. Not their learning. Not their potential. That is for somewhere else. The group says No! to learning and possibilities. Those are nice things, maybe, but probably not. It is not about your learning. It is not about the best way to serve a purpose other than the boss's goal. What the group is here to do. It is only about the outcomes. It is not about learning. It is not about evolving as a group. It's only about getting the job done. It's about taking what we already know and telling the group how they are going to do it. It is saying No! to your interpretation of what the group might do, to your creativity about what the group might do. It is saying No! to the purpose. It is about getting the job done, with the capacities at hand. It is about doing what is in the book. The given rules. It starts and ends with a No!

So, taking all those elements together = saying Yes! to me and my learning and growth, to you and your learning and growth, to the group's capacity to learn and grow, to the creative process for seeing and manifesting something, getting the feedback and adjusting, evolving over time, saying Yes! to the creativity that has been received from before, what is in the book, and to learning and interpreting. That all of you can do that. Saying Yes!

to a greater purpose. This is saying Yes! to a future you love. Saying Yes! to something that you care deeply about. Saying Yes! to love. Yes! to life. Yes! to human creativity.

No is saying No! to all of that. Saying No! is starting with the belief that there isn't any. With scarcity. Saying No! to life. No! to love. It is saying No! to the future. There is no future that you love, to which you will give your will. It is about doing what is here right now, only. No! to love. No! to life. No! to human creativity.

ONE EXPERIENCE

All these things happen in your Yes!, your No!, in the net positive, or the net negative. Because it is one experience. It is one system. The outcomes you achieve, the experience you have, all that happens when you interact. And you interact with other human beings, with other roles, with yourself, with other elements in nature, with resources.

When you interact—interactions with each other—you experience it as something inwardly. You experience, and you achieve outcomes. Something happens because of that. Those are all at the same time. These interactions that you have are with different nodes, with different elements, with different people. These interactions, or links, between these two nodes, two different beings, are based on agreements. Based on how you agree that you will be in this relationship. This information will inform the decisions made, as you interact with others.

The agreements that you make are based on underlying assumptions. Assumptions of how you see the world, and what you think an agreement can be. In some of these agreements (which you will see later were implicit, meaning you do not see them) you are not clear what the agreements even are, in the moment. Or, some are explicit, and they are codified. They are known.

The assumptions underlying agreements are indeed unconscious. So, if you are having these assumptions about reality that drive the kinds of agreements you have, about how you interact with something, and that drives your experiences and outcomes in understanding these different elements, it becomes critical to determine whether you are starting with a Yes!. Whether you are being in the Yes!, and whether what you are doing is resulting in a Yes!.

Meaning that these outcomes, experiences, interactions, agreements, and assumptions are all happening at the same time, in the same place, and that is the exciting, powerful thing.

If you are not getting the outcomes or experiences you want, you believe you can do better. If you want there to be a Yes! consistent throughout, you have different elements that you can explore. I can shift different elements to help you achieve what you want. Where is the Yes!? Where is the No!? This can happen because it is all one experience. All one domain, all at the same time. While that might seem obvious, most people do not act this way, most of the time.

People tend to focus on looking at outcomes, in a different time and space than they are right now, and forget what experiences and interactions drove those outcomes. Meaning they are not very good at looking back, at understanding what drove them to what they are experiencing now. They forget and they do not equate the quality of their experience with the outcomes that they are achieving. They do not equate the quality of their outer experiences with the underlying agreements they have about interactions, and they do not look to see that they have a lot of assumptions about what these agreements could be, from an economic, political, cultural, or social perspective. They do not see what things they are interacting with. They do not see who decides and enforces. They do not see what criteria they use, and they do not see where the rules of the game are explicit or implicit while they are interacting and having these experiences that achieve these outcomes. So, it is realizing the power. It is realizing that these elements are all in the same space at the same time, and this is how you can start to dig into your Yes!, your Yes! to love, to life.

Let's say you were working on preparing a dinner party together. You can have some friends over for dinner. In the afternoon, you are working on that together. You enjoy cohosting the party together. You are pretty good at getting things done, in helping in the kitchen, and you like to cook and help run errands. He likes decorating and she is a really good cook. So, we interact. We are working with each other to create this dinner and the environment for the party, the setting. That leads us to the outcome of when people arrive. Dinner is ready, as is the dinner environment. You also have an experience, while doing that. Is that fun? Are you better? Is your relationship better because you did this together? Or are you worse off and stressed out because you did this together? You are interacting, and you have both the experience and the outcomes, the experience of doing the dinner preparation together, and the outcome of what it looks like when we are done.

This is based on a set of agreements that determine how we interact, and these agreements have some assumptions underneath them. The economic question of, "What resources do you see?" Does it look to you like there are the resources of ingredients for the meal and the preparations for the room only? Or do the available resources also include your capacity to learn, try things, and adjust with each other? Do you also see resources of how you think about what you could try and what you could see in how you work on that together, while learning, as well as the resources that you have at hand in the moment: the ingredients, the party favors, the room, the cutlery, the table settings, and decorations.

The political question of, "Who decides?" You can decide who is going to decide, and how you are going to enforce decisions. You can decide whether that is something that you decide for the group. Or something that you and others decide together. Or something that you call other people for input on. Do you decide some things, and others decide some things? Are you supporting another in trying to figure out what you might want to do here, and you are working with them to see what they are learning? And if you are understanding how things are working? There are so many levels that you can look at in these questions of who decides and who enforces.

You have the cultural question of, "What values do you use to decide?" What are the criteria you use? Do you value more that you must get an outcome? Or that you get the outcome, and you have a good time learning, developing, and trying things to make it beautiful! Or are you looking at values of the potential, and could you create something new together? How you are learning and developing your capacities, as you are doing it and the experiencing outcome of what you have created.

And then what are the rules of your interactions? The social question. "What are the rules of the game?" Is this a thing where you each go do your own thing, or are there some things that you do together, and then the rest is on your own? Or are you continuously working in creating this together? These very different assumptions about how you will interact determine what you see is possible in the experience you have. In the outcomes you achieve.

This observation can be generalized. ISC has been working on it for the past 16 years. With our friends, our colleagues, our networks of projects, in dozens of countries around the globe, as well as our survey in 126 different countries.

1000S OF LEADERS IN 100S OF GROUPS HAVE CHOSEN TO SHIFT

ISC's network has found thousands of leaders and hundreds of groups that have chosen their Yes! They have chosen to shift their agreements towards much greater engagement, much greater impact. Towards their Yes!

For example, in a group I worked closely with for over 10 years, it started by looking around the room one day and observing, "We like this group. We enjoy each other. Are we achieving what we know we can?" We know what we are achieving, and we know what is ours to do. Is this our Big Yes!? We found that our answer was, not really. With that clarity, we set out to try to see how we could shift our experiences and our interactions with each other.

What are the underlying agreements and assumptions that we have around how we actually interact? We have words that we say that we think are important in how we make our decisions and how we see the resources and the criteria we use in how we interact. The four big economic, political, cultural, and social questions. But is that what we actually do? What are the actual behaviors, the actual assumptions that we are operating with, at any given moment, in our interactions? What experiences are we actually having? What outcomes are we actually achieving? Can we put all those together on the same page? See if we are achieving these outcomes and having these experiences, in these interactions. If we can see what we are actually doing, then maybe these are the actual assumptions that we have versus our stated ones. If we can see that, with the clarity of what we actually want, then we can start to shift what we do, and we can try to do that on a more regular basis.

A friend leading a software engineering group within a large financial institution asked the same questions. Are we achieving the outcomes and experiences that we want? If not, then how can we change our interactions and how we see the world to get different outcomes and experiences? She was able to negotiate the freedom to work with her group, over a few years, to see what would happen. To "evaluate me and the group based solely on the outcomes. Measure my success based on whether I am getting the outcomes that you know this group can achieve, compared with what they are now. I will go and look at and work on the underlying assumptions that we all have. How those assumptions influence the agreements that we make. How we interact, and the experiences we have over time, in this very large company". She was able to begin to shift the underlying assumptions that everyone brought to work into their interactions every day, and all their work around what was available. How decisions were made by me, by you, by us, in the creative process. The political question. What we valued. What we held as a criterion for how we were making decisions in every moment. The cultural question. How we came together to do these things. The social question. What we saw as the resources available to us. The economic question. By making this all explicit, they were able to see that it led to very different interactions. Much more engaged experiences. To far better results. By focusing on all of this, she was able to shift the group towards much greater encouragement, much greater impact, much further towards their Yes! for each individual and the group.

One last example, from a Latin America network of extraordinary leaders coming together, who have each achieved huge successes in their own realms, their own networks and communities. Achievements recognized locally, nationally, and globally. They are coming together, as a network, to see if they can achieve together something at the national and global level that they have not been able to achieve before on their own as individuals. They looked at what they held to be true. At the resources that they have. How they make decisions amongst themselves, not within each of their networks, but amongst themselves. Me and you and us, in the creative process. What they actually value. The criteria that they use in making each of those decisions. How they interact. Their rules of the game. They saw that they knew that what they had to achieve is a far higher level of outcomes and engagement than they were achieving right then, even as successful as they each were on their own. Now they had to come together. What are the steps that they each need to take, individually and as a group, to be able to do that? They are now taking those first steps, seeing what they are learning as they try, in their movement, in their underlying agreements, in the assumptions that they carry. In the interacting experiences they are actually having, they are seeing the outcomes that they are achieving. They are seeing how it all tells them one story. Their story. Of their assumptions, their agreements, their interactions, their experience, and their outcomes. One story of their Yes!

LESSONS LEARNED

There has been a strong response to Yes! over the last 19 years. My group has worked in 59 countries, trying this out. This is a community of people coming together around ecosynomics, abundance-based approaches to looking at their own agreements, sharing what they are learning, what they are trying, and how they can shift together.

This is combined with ISC´S survey research in 126 countries. Over one hundred and ninety five thousand people have used the survey to express and explore the experience of their agreements. The free, online Agreements Health Check survey is available to you at isclarity.org.

What we have learned from this is that people can say Yes! They are able to ground this Yes! in practice. They are able to say Yes! To choose to see their agreements. To do this together. To choose together to align their agreements. To align their agreements with their underlying assumptions. How they actually interact. The experience that they have. What it feels like, and the outcomes they achieve. To realize that this is all the same package. They can choose these agreements. They can use them together.

You can align all these elements, and then you can start to shift. You can implement this. You can see that you have assumptions that influence the interactions you have. You can test what you believe. These are assumptions. Look at how your interactions actually work. What you actually do in your interactions. Are those consistent with the assumptions you think you have? What assumptions do you actually have when you operate versus your stated ones? Do you say you are cooperative and appreciate cooperation, then find that you do things on your own? Do you say that listening is very important, then observe that you do not listen? Or that you do sometimes, and do not sometimes? What are the differences that you experience of why you have different assumptions?

Are the assumptions different in different groups? You can start the test to see what the underlying assumptions are that you have in different settings. How does that lead to different agreements about your interactions? Does that lead to different experiences and outcomes in the different places and groups where you work?

You can start to see these agreements. You can start to choose. If that is what is happening, what else could happen? Can you start to align your outcomes and experiences, interactions, agreements, assumptions with your Big Yes!? With what you know is yours to do. What you know is ours to do. To the level of what you know we are able to achieve.

You can learn how to improve this over time, using processes like they do in agile software. Prototyping. Let's go try. Now that you started to describe all this as one instance, one system, one whole, you can observe what happens when you start to shift the different elements of this one whole.

What if, instead of thinking of what is available to you right now, an underlying economic assumption thinking only about the capacities or resources that you already have right here, you started to include what you are learning. Maybe you are thinking about something new you saw today. You are learning. You can ask, "What surprised me in the last week?" Then you can start to ask questions.

If you believe that the questions are important, how will you begin to look at your day, your week, your interactions with another? Will you come in telling another what to do, or will you come in asking? If you are asking, then who is deciding? Do you ask with a statement, telling another what their answer should be, or do you ask and actually listen?

Then you must decide how you do that. You can support another in feeling that it is okay and trusting that it is okay to share what each other is learning. Then you can listen to and work with what the others are learning and what you are learning. You can see how that affects your outcomes. How it affects the resources that you see that you have available. You can do that in your decision making, because you are starting to realize that you value what is being learned. The new capacities developing in addition to those that you already have. That you are starting to cooperate, to bring together what you are doing and what others are doing into the same space, at the same time. That is just an example of starting to implement, to adjust, to evolve.

What is evolution here? Evolution is realizing that you are starting with how you see the world, and then something happens, and now you see it differently. You have this amazing thing happen in your reality called feedback. You see something and you think about it. You see something new. You see a way that you can maybe test what you see. You then see an action that you can take. A verb. Then you can see what happens.

When you do that and see the feedback, you observe a sacred noun. Wow! Look at what happened. It is not an error. It is not about whether you were right or wrong. Rather, you went and tried an experiment, and now you have data. With the data you now have of what happened, what actually do you now see about how the world works?

Now you can begin to think about what to try next. How does what you observed happening change what you saw as a possibility? How does it shift the way you saw to try it, the verb? What do you see now, as a possibility, as a way to test it? Learning from the feedback, you have shifted what you think, what you see as possible, what you are going to try next, looking for your next outcome. This is evolution. Continuously learning from what the feedback of the universe is telling you and adjusting. You can do this over the short term and over the long term. What is it you are here to do right now? How does that align with what you are here to do in the longer term? How does that align with your big Yes! in the longer-term? Yes.

These are all simple examples of the Yes! Saying what is your Yes!, what you know to be true. What are these initial conditions that you are bringing to it? What does that lead to?

As we have seen, when you start from Yes! and align with your Yes!, the experience and outcomes are very different. You can align the Yes! in your assumptions with the Yes! in your agreements. With the Yes! in your interactions. With the Yes! you want in your experience, and the Yes! in your outcomes and impacts. When you start to align all of these, then those are the initial conditions of your Yes!

That is what we discovered in our research with hundreds of these groups, from around the world, and from our survey in all these 126 countries over the last 18 years. When you start from Yes!, you start with Yes! in all these levels of your assumptions, your agreements, your interactions, your experiences, your outcomes. The result is always net positive. You always generate far more value than it takes to do this work.

Where you find a No! in your assumptions, your agreements, your interactions, your experiences, your outcomes, the result is always net negative. You generate less value than it costs to do this.

So, the question is, "Do you want net positive or net negative results?" Whether you get net positive or net negative is contingent on your initial conditions. On your Yes!

Is it a thorough Yes! or a partial Yes!? Or not really a Yes!? Whenever you accept not saying Yes!, you are accepting a No! You accept the No! into your assumptions, your interactions, your experiences, and your outcomes. Whenever you accept this No!, you end up in net negative.

If you start with a Yes! and if you can align, then you can see the Yes! You can choose the Yes!, and you can implement it. You can adjust. You can evolve. As all these groups continuously demonstrate. It is straightforward for human beings to do. And they do. That is the human creative act. You can say Yes!, and the result of that is always net positive.

ALL LEVELS FOR ALL YESES!

When I started to realize that the world was based on these agreements that we have in our assumptions, interactions, experiences, and outcomes, I started to realize that there was more than just one world. I realized that, for many years, I had been teaching, acting, and leading from an assumption that scarcity, that No!, was the only reality. It was a reality that I was constantly fighting to try to get more out of. I wanted to get more out of it, in service to what I cared about.

Then we started to find groups that were very different. We came upon individuals, groups, communities, teams, companies, and networks that were able to achieve much higher levels of engagement, experiences, outcomes, and impacts.We started to realize that they had very different ways of interacting with each other, based on very different agreements and assumptions. As we started to clarify what we were seeing, and then what we were looking for, we quickly started to see more and more of these groups. Now it is far into thousands that we have found and worked with, in all these countries since the early 2000s.

We started to realize there is actually a continuum, from very, very basic levels of understanding of our agreements and our underlying assumptions to very high levels. There is not just one world. It is not that you are either doing it from scarcity or abundance. There is not only one way to engage in the world, rather there is a whole continuum.

At the level of the basics, you can agree that these are the resources you have. You will assign someone to be the boss, to decide. You can use the efficiency of the organization. You can measure your profitability or the use of these funds to get access to the services you need for a government agency. For this team, this is the job to do. Go do it. And that is how you agree to work together. A very basic level of agreements. If you are aware of it, and align around it, it can still be healthy. You deliver great service or a great product because you know what you are doing. You have the resources. You are efficient and effective at doing the work.

My group has also found people who are choosing to shift from the basics level of agreements to agreements of learning organizations. In these groups, they are starting to realize that maybe they can learn from what they are doing. Over time, they start to see that learning is also important. They start to make time and space for supporting each other in learning. They make time for mentoring, and different kinds of processes that support their learning and developing capacities and relationships over time. Some decide some of those things for the group, as the boss, and others decide other things. Some decide those things for themselves, and what they are learning. Others can support them in that learning because what they are valuing is the learning. They adjust over time, and how that adds to the value of what they can achieve over time.

We also find groups shifting from the cooperative level of learning agreements to the collaborative level of agreements. People are moving from learning on their own and appreciating the other to bringing shared resources together to starting to work out of the same resources towards the same goals. Starting to work much more deeply together. They begin to focus on what one is learning, what another is learning, and what they are learning together. How that is developing their capacity to see further into what they can do. What it is that they value. How they come together in their clarity of what they are trying to achieve. What they are learning over time. The resources and networks that they need to be able to do that. How they create space and time for their working and another's working and the group's working. In the outcomes that they get, at all those levels. How that affects what they can see and adjust.

We are also seeing people move from the high-performing collaborative level of agreements to the deep-collaboration level of agreements. What does it mean to imagine together? In their Yes!, they are in this work together, in service of what they are trying to achieve. That deeper, shared purpose is important, as well as what they are learning and developing, as they are moving into that service, trying things, and achieving outcomes now.

It is not that one of these levels replaces the others, rather that each one of these levels shifts how you see the earlier level. At each level, you still want and keep outcomes, so the outcomes are still important. You add learning. Then you add potential. Then you add the process of seeing potential and learning, which the outcomes inform.

In these shifts, you can begin to ask, "Why do you really need each other?" What are the kinds of processes that can break through how you listen to each other at a much deeper level, to what is common that you all hold, that you really need each other for, that you need to be able to work through the diversity of your perspectives, so that you can achieve something far greater that you know is yours to do together?

What this means is that these are all levels for all Yeses!, from basics to learning organizations. From cooperative communities to collaborative forms. From very high-performing collaboratives to deep collaboration from love to sacred hospitality. These are all different levels. The agreements at each are very different.

The underlying assumptions lead to different agreements and interactions with very different experiences and very different outcomes. They are all levels of Yes!, and they are all available to you.

People around the world are figuring this out, all the time. They are not Olympians, meaning that they are not perfect human beings who are able to do something the rest cannot. It is part of human nature to be able to do this. The question is what you know about your Yes! Are you starting with a Yes!? Are you aligning yourself to that Yes! and all these dimensions, by trying and seeing and celebrating what you are learning! Or are you accepting the No!? All these levels of Yes! are available to you. All of these are forms of your Yes! You can see where you are, and move upwards on this continuum, towards an ever bigger Yes! It depends on what you know is yours to do, your Yes!

WHAT ARE AGREEMENTS?

HOW DO I KNOW WHEN I AM IN AN AGREEMENT?

You have seen that you start with a Yes! or a No!, and that has an impact. My group has identified thousands of groups, across the world, who are learning to live from Yes! We also saw that there is a whole continuum, from No! to Yes!

So now we will look at what you know about your agreements. How do you know when you are in an agreement? Why do you prefer some agreements more? How can you start thinking about applying this in your everyday life?

How do you know when you are in an agreement? One answer is simple. You are always in an agreement. Everything you do is an interaction. You are always interacting, within yourself, with other parts of yourself. You are always interacting with other human beings. You are interacting with nature to live, as a verb. Verbs are interactions, movement through. When you interact, you are in an agreement. That suggests that maybe you are always in an agreement.

The question is, do you know what agreement you are in, and what are the conditions of this agreement? You looked at this before. At the assumptions, interactions, experience, and outcomes. Are those conditions aligned with what you are in service to, with your Big Yes!? Or are you accepting a No!?

Maybe you are always in an agreement. You do not have to accept that from me. You do not have to believe that to be true. You can see for yourself.

Another way you know you are in an agreement is that all agreements have purposeful energy. Physics, biology, and chemistry tell you that the world is energy. Everything that has mass, and even the dark matter between the units of mass, has energy. The whole thing is energy.

Looking deeper into what energy is, we find that energy, by its nature, is always transforming, changing from one form to another. The word energy comes from the Greek *energeia*, with the roots *en* for "at" and *ergon* for "work" or "action", thus energy is the capacity to perform work, to change from one form to another, to transform. When you lift a rock higher into the air, you convert mechanical energy to potential energy. It has potential energy, meaning that if you let go of it, it converts potential energy into the kinetic energy of movement energy, and it has an impact when it falls. As it falls and when it falls.

There is always energy, and everything is energy. As the physicists, chemists, and biologists tell us, everything is some form of energy. As Einstein simplified with $E=mc^2$, if it has mass, it is energy.

If there is always energy, and it is always moving and transforming, then it is transforming toward something. The question is whether you know what that something is. There is a debate on whether life has a purpose or not. At some level, you can start to understand that everything is moving toward something, whether you want to think of that as divine purpose or some other person's purpose. Whether this thing knows that it is doing that or not. But let's take all that away, for the moment, and just say that it is transforming toward something.

If you do not know what it is moving towards, then it is moving towards some thing without your choice. Without your alignment. If you know what it is moving towards, then you can choose to align yourself with that. You can choose to agree with what it is moving towards. You can be in an agreement with it.

You know when you are in agreement. In any context that you are interacting in, which is all of them, all the time, then you are in some form of an agreement. Agreement with the conditions for that interaction. Everything has purposeful energy, meaning energy that is moving toward something, which energy always is because it is always transforming. This is the definition of the nature of energy. In moving towards another form, it is moving toward some purpose, toward some thing. When that happens, then there is a "towards." There is an organizing principle, a towards that organizes the context and the movement towards another form. In this situation, you are in an agreement, in an underlying set of assumptions that are guiding the interactions of that movement. In all of that, you are in an agreement. Do you know you are in an agreement? If you do, then you can choose how you are in that agreement.

WHY DO I PREFER SOME AGREEMENTS MORE?

Realizing that you are in an agreement, always, and that there is energy moving toward something, then you can start to understand those agreements. Realizing this, the second question you can ask is, "Why do I prefer some agreements more?" Do you prefer certain kinds of agreements? From our research, we discover that people know the difference. You know when you experience being in agreements that you do not like. Where you have an experience you do not appreciate. That you do not want to be in. That you want to get out of. Outcomes that you do not agree with.

You also experience agreements that you do like. Outcomes that you do want. Experiences that you do enjoy.

We started all this by saying that this is part of what it feels like when it is your Yes! or your No! What we are starting to realize is that some agreements are more towards your Yes!, and others are more towards your No! You have different ways that you know what you prefer. You can look at this from four very simple perspectives. You can look at this from the level of your experience. I have asked tens of thousands of people to describe their experiences. I hear the following in all of them. You can do the same—ask others what they know from their own experience.

Informal Survey. Think about your own experiences. When you think about a really great group, what is the experience that you have? You know the difference between the experiences that you prefer and the experiences you don't. What are some of those characteristics? Write some down.

My colleagues and I have done this exercise with hundreds of groups in dozens of countries. Through the free Agreements Health Check survey, we have asked people in 126 countries. We find the following. People love to experience higher levels of the harmonic in how they interact. There is much more harmony there. It all seems to come together. All the voices come together to generate something else. There is a harmonic that everyone seems to really appreciate.

My colleague Professor Tim Lomas has found expressions of harmony and balance in cultures around the world. Everyone knows what it is and has developed vocabulary to explore it and describe it. There is another level of vibrancy, experienced in what they value. More value feels more vibrant. We have found this in many cultures, in many languages. Some form of talking about the vibe of a group. The *vibra* in Spanish. People everywhere describe an experience of something that vibrates at a higher level. There is much greater vibrancy experienced through what they value, through what they appreciate of what is available to them.

They prefer agreements where there is more power in who decides and enforces the decision. Where it feels like there is more power to do something in the world. For example, in your agreements, does one person have all the power to decide, or do some people have that power? Or do many of us have the power? When people describe more vibrant experiences, they talk about there being more power available to do something. They can access that energy—they have the power—to do something with it.

They prefer agreements where they experience more abundance in what is available. There is more available in the resources they have. There is more available in the learning and opening up to new relationships and capacities. There is more abundance in the possibilities, in the developing, and in the actual resources and content that they have available to them right now.

Simple way that you know	What you prefer in your experience	Lens
Harmonic	Greater harmonics available through your social interactions	Social
Vibrancy	Greater vibrancy in the presence of what you value	Cultural
Power	Greater power in who decides and enforces decisions that involve you	Political
Abundance	Greater abundance of the resources visible and accessible to you	Economic

These are four simple ways for knowing what you prefer in your experience. In any experience you can ask yourself, are you better because you were here, in this situation, with these people, or are you worse off? Returning to what we observed earlier, when you start with love, when you start with Yes! to life, to human creativity, to love, the net result is always positive. You are always better off.

It is hard work. It takes a lot. There are many challenges. There might be difficult moments. And the net result is always positive. This is what people report and share from all their experiences. When you are in agreements with a low harmonic, of low vibrancy, of low power, of low abundance or scarcity, then you experience that the net result is negative.

So, why do you prefer some agreements more? Because these agreements bring a greater level of harmonic in how you interact. There is a greater vibrancy in what you value. You have access to more power to do something with this purposeful energy. You experience greater abundance, in the resources that are available to you, for potential, for developing capacities, and the capacities you have. You experience more of these things in certain kinds of agreements. You prefer agreements that have more than agreements that have less.

EXAMPLE

You are the CEO. Often people understand a CEO to be the Chief Executive Officer, like in a company. That is not what a CEO really is. CEO really means the Chooser of Experiences and Outcomes. You are the CEO of your life. The one who chooses the experiences and outcomes you have, the designer of your life.

What does this mean for you? Let's look at designing your life. What does designing your life look like? My colleague Hernando Aguilera takes us on a brief journey of designing your life.

In essence, it is a simple, five-step process. Start with your experience in a group or space. Do you experience greater scarcity or greater abundance? Connect that experience with the dimensions of your life that are in service to your purpose. Explore the experience in your primary relationships, with your own self, the other, the group, nature's creative process, and spirit's creative source. Understand how the agreements in the context of your experience have embedded assumptions, which can be seen through economic, political, cultural, and social lenses. You can then begin to map how to align your agreements with your purpose. Hernando's group works through each of these five steps, one per week, over a five-week period. This allows everyone to both take the time to observe what is happening in their lives with each question, and to work through these questions together. Working together gives you multiple perspectives on your own experiences, and a community to work through the steps. A commitment device.

Let's look at each of the five steps to designing your life in a little more detail.

Step #1. Your experience

Thinking about a specific group, do you feel more engaged or less? Do you feel like you're learning and more of you shows up or less? Do you feel like you are better, smarter, more engaged because of the time you spent with the group, or worse, with fewer ideas, less engaged, and ready to not be with the group?

Your purpose. What is your deeper purpose? What guides what you say Yes! to? What are some of the purposes that you give your intention and attention to, in service to that purpose? What does that purpose look like for other key roles you have in your life? As a family member, as a friend, as a colleague, as a citizen?

All these areas of your experience happen in the same experience. As you saw earlier in the book, your underlying assumptions influence the agreements you choose and those that you accept. These agreements influence how you interact with others. These interactions influence experiences you have and the outcomes you achieve. The feedback from these experiences and outcomes allows you to see how well your assumptions and agreements support what you are trying to do, in service to your deeper purpose, in the many roles you have in your life. You can use this feedback to adjust your assumptions and agreements, aligning them with your purpose, with what happens in your interactions.

A key insight in Step #1 is to realize that you have an experience, and that you can know that you are having that experience. You can feel it. Ask yourself how you know. Where do you feel that? What does it feel like? How do you interpret that? It turns out that we each do this differently. We each bring a unique set of ways of perceiving and interpreting what is happening. To align your agreements with your purpose, you are designing your life. To do this, you can calibrate what you experience, how you experience it, and how you perceive that experience.

Step #2. Your Reality

The second step looks at your reality. How you perceive reality. As described earlier in the book, there are three basic levels of perceived reality with which most people engage in life. The level of tangible things, the outcomes from what you did before. The already-finished. The nouns in your awareness. There is also the level of movement, of developing new capacities and relationships. The verbs in your awareness of what is happening right here and right now, in the present. The third level is the level of potential, where possibilities live. This is where you see new things, from the future. You might see a new possibility and a pathway to manifesting it, to making it also-real.

What are daily experiences you have of each of these levels, in your own experience? These are not abstract ideas of philosophers, rather experiences you have all day long. Looking at specific agreements that you have, with specific groups, do you and the group tend to focus more on one of these levels of perceived reality? More on the outcomes, and much less on learning and possibilities? Look at what levels you tend to focus on in the different groups you engage with, and in the different roles you have in your daily life.

A key insight from Step #2 is that your agreements tend to come from and support specific levels of perceived reality. What can then happen in your interactions, experiences, and outcomes is influenced, in great part, by the levels of reality that you allow in, consciously, through your agreements.

Step #3. Your Primary Relations

The third step in designing your life explores the level of vibrancy you experience in a given set of agreements, using as the tool your experience in your five primary relationships. How much of you shows up? The capacities you already bring, your learning and development, your deeper evolution? In your relationship with the other, do you experience being seen and seeing others for their capacities, supporting others in learning, supporting each other in the vulnerability of deep growth? In the capacities anybody brings to the group, working as a group together, inviting the contributions of all unique perspectives required to serve the purpose? Do the creative processes of the group focus on outcomes only, learning and outcomes, or seeing possibilities while learning and achieving outcomes? Does the group's creativity come from what was already received from the past, what is in the book, or what can be interpreted by some creative experts, or do they see the creativity in received wisdom and in their experts and in everyone everywhere? These are five primary ways that you relate to your experience, through the self, the other, the group, nature's creative process of innovation, and spirit's source of creativity.

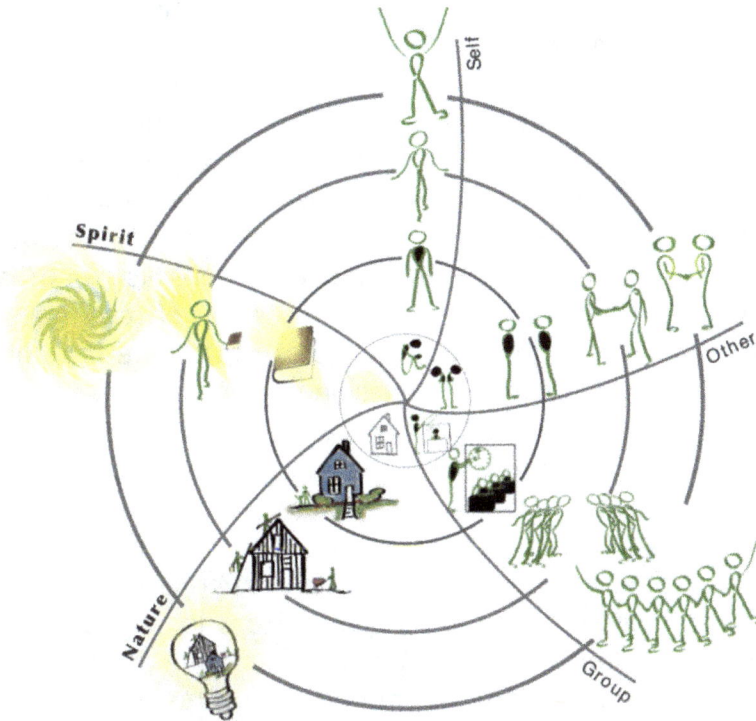

Figure 1: Three Levels in Five Primary Relationships

The key insight from Step #3 is the coherence in levels of experience across all five primary relationships. Evidence shows that where a group's agreements support higher levels of experience in your relationship to your own self, you also experience higher levels in your relationship to the other, to the group, to the creative process, and to the source of creativity. Where you experience lower levels in any of these primary relationships, you also experience lower levels in the other primary relationships. The Institute for Strategic Clarity has found this to be consistent from over 196,000 people describing their experiences of the five primary relationships.

Step #4. Four Lenses on Your World

The fourth step looks at your agreements in each of the three levels of perceived reality (nouns, verbs, possibilities) through four basic lenses that have existed in all cultures for at least the past few millennia. Thinking again of that specific group, how much is there available to you and the resources you use? Do you see, typically, only the tangible things or also the learning and developing resources, such as mentoring and asking questions, and do you see the possibility resources for exploring the yet unknown? This is the economic lens. Who decides and who enforces those decisions in this group? Is it the same for all decisions, for all allocation of resources, or does it depend on the specific process instead of relationships, or does it bring in specific decision power depending on the predominant primary relationship at any given moment? This is the political lens. What criteria are used to decide and enforce, at any given moment? Are the values based on outcomes only, or also on learning and developing, and criteria for what is emerging, what is new? This is the cultural lens. What are the rules of the game? How do people interact with the resources and each other? Each one on their own, competing with the others, or pooling resources to cooperate on specific activities, or collaborating deeply, each contributing their unique perspective towards a deeper shared purpose? This is the social lens.

The key insight from step #4 is that you have four very well-developed lenses that you can use to describe a specific experience, a specific set of agreements. Maybe these areas of study (economics, politics, culture, sociology) are not four different things but rather four different perspectives on one thing. When you see them as different things, typically you then see at least one of the other perspectives as irrelevant. When you see them as four lenses on your experience, they can each contribute valuable insights about your world. They ask different, complementary questions.

Step #5. Your Agreements Mapping

The fifth step, in this initial foray into designing your life, looks for specific evidence in these agreements you have. Looking for what you can see as real evidence in your life, through each lens, look at each level of perceived reality. What exists? What is missing? What might you try next? How might you try that?

The key insight from step #5 is that there is evidence in your life, which you can see and map. These are evidence of your agreements. Your actual agreements and your potential agreements. What you are doing now, and what you could try now. Again, it is your choice. And that is the point. It is your life. You are the Chooser of Experiences and Outcomes in your life, the CEO. The designer of your life.

Once again, a deep hat tip to Hernando and his community for continuing to find simple, clear and immediately actionable ways of working with your agreements, using the tools, with simple instructions.

As you work on your agreements, designing your life, you might want to be able to assess where you are in your agreements at any given time, as experienced through the vibrancy in your five primary relationships.

YOUR AGREEMENTS HEALTH PORTAL

You might have a blood-pressure monitor or know how to check your pulse. You probably have a thermometer to check your body's temperature when you suspect you might have a fever. These are ways to check your physical health, how well your biological body is working.

You can do the same for your agreements, for the experience your relational body has in your interactions. To check the health of your agreements, the Institute for Strategic Clarity created the Agreements Health Check. Through the Institute's free, online Agreements Health Portal (isclarity.org), you can register to track the health of your agreements, in any group you want, as often as you want. Check the health of your agreements in a specific group, periodically, and test the health of your agreements in different groups. You can also register to invite your groups to look at the health of their agreements together. This is all completely confidential.

The Agreements Health Check takes about 8 minutes to assess whether your agreements are low, medium, or high. Whether they start with a No! or with a Yes! The Agreements Health Check looks at how much you experience No! or Yes! in the agreements with your own self, with another person, with the group, with the creative process, and with the source of creativity.

When you see where you are, according to the frequency you report what you experience in your agreements, you can see if that aligns with what it feels like for you. This is your first clue. You can know what it feels like to be in a set of agreements, an agreements field, because you have a sensory perception organ for this. You know what it feels like. You know what it feels like to be in a weak agreements field, or in a strong agreements field. The Agreements Health Check is a way of calibrating your interpretation of the input from your sensory perception organ. This is what it feels like, and this is the health of that agreements field.

Combining your own, subjective sensing with the objective assessment of the Agreements Health Check, you can start to see what choices you have, in the experiences of the relationship with your own self, with others, with the group, with nature's creative process, and with spirit's source of creativity.

Here is what the output of your Agreements Health Check looks like. I just used it to look at the agreements in a group I am working with right now.

ISC Agreements Health Check Survey

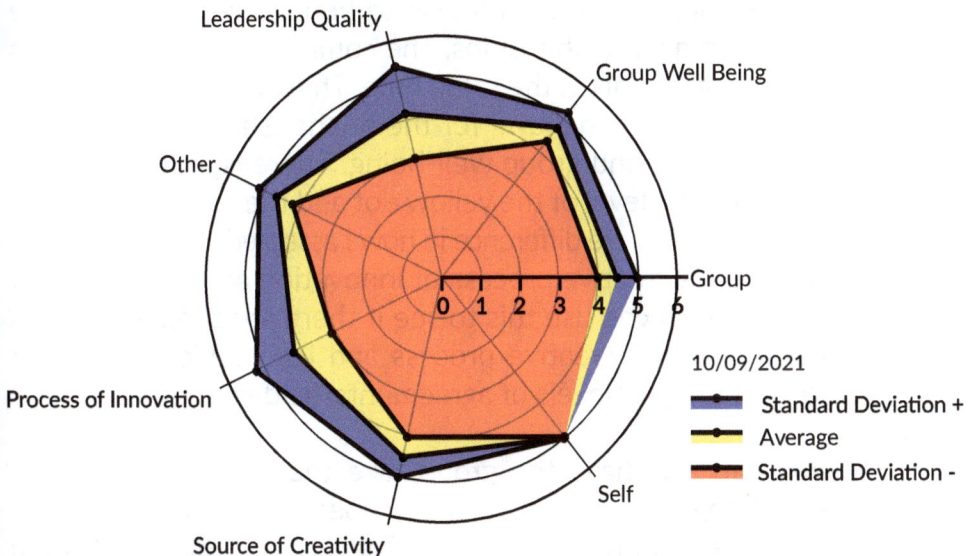

Figure 2: Agreements Health Portal

This spider diagram summarizes your Agreements Health, on seven dimensions. The five primary relationships just described (self, other, group, nature, spirit), as well as the perceived well-being of the group and the quality of leadership. The yellow points show you the strength of each dimension of your agreements health, as an average of the different sub-dimensions you assessed. The blue and red points, for each dimension, show you the range of your responses for that dimension, using plus and minus one standard deviation for the assessment of that dimension.

On a first pass, this specific Agreements Health Check shows me three things. First, it shows that the overall level is between the middle and outer circles, in the 4 range. This shows an agreements field that is strong in developing and outcomes, building capacities into the realm of possibilities. This level correlates with what you saw as a strong agreements field in earlier chapters, able to engage, transform, and transfer much of the available energy and human creativity. Second, this Agreements Health Check summary shows that there is a relatively coherent level of agreements across all these dimensions: they are all at close to the same level. This means that the agreements support higher levels of abundance, power, vibrancy, and harmonic to be experienced in all five of the primary relationships. The common set of agreements support all of this at the same time. Third, my responses were mostly at the same level for the relationships to self, other, group, spirit, and group well-being. There is little difference between the level of the yellow dot and the blue and red dots. There is a bit more difference in how I assessed the relationships to nature's creative process of innovation and the quality of leadership. I can use this to see if there are specific aspects of the group's creative process and leadership that reflect lower or higher levels of agreements-field strength.

You can also have the group take the Agreements Health Check together. Each person describes their experience of the agreements of the same group. The assessment provides you with an assessment of how the group assesses each dimension, on average, and how much agreement there is or not on that assessment. In the following output from the assessment, the vertical axis is the average score for all the questions, on the same 1-5 scale, and the horizontal axis is the standard deviation, across the group, of their assessment of the frequency at which they experience that question. Overall, this figure shows that most of the group's responses are in the blue region, where they score it high, and there is general agreement on that. The white region shows that are three responses where there were either lower average scores or there was a bit of divergence in the assessment of those questions. The yellow regions show that there are four responses where the average score was either low or assessments were quite varied.

Avg.: 4.50, StDev.: 0.66

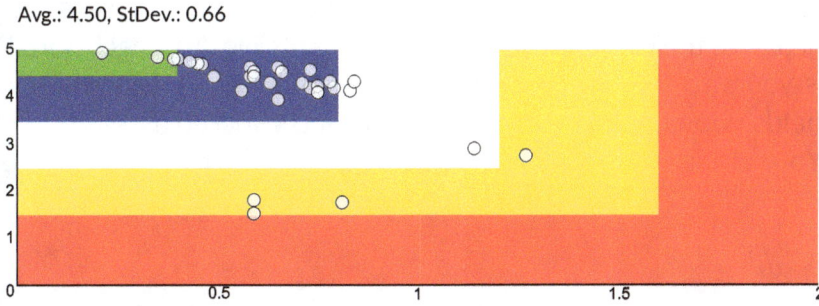

Figure 3: Agreements Health Check of a Group

The assessment then goes on to provide details of which responses ended up in each of these color regions. I use this assessment to guide explorations of where there is agreement on the experience, and what might be underlying the perceived differences in experience. This exploration is usually very enlightening. Particularly in two areas of exploration. First, it is interesting to explore what the group does, in its structures and practices, to support the stronger agreements. Many times, the group is not aware of what specifically enables these experiences. Being explicit allows the group to agree that they indeed support those practices, see what is needed to continue to engage those healthier practices, and to see if they might even improve on those practices. Until the practices are made explicit, you cannot explore these questions. Second, it is also interesting to explore the differences in perception of the same experience. Often it is a difference in expectations and relative experience. While Fred thought the group was quite attentive to others' perspectives, Maria thought it was not. Inquiry showed that Fred was comparing the group to his other main working group, which was much less attentive. Relatively, this group was doing great! Maria was comparing the group's actual attentiveness with what she thought they were capable of doing. She expected even more from herself and her colleagues. Exploring both perspectives, they saw that they agreed where they thought they diverged. They were looking at the experience in relation to different experiences. They felt this exploration enriched their understanding of their group and of how each other reacted within those experiences.

Join the over 196,000 people who have used it to assess the health of their agreements. The Agreements Health Check portal is yours to use. For your own assessment of the agreements fields you engage in, and for your group's shared assessment. Your choice.

WHAT ARE AGREEMENTS FIELDS?

SCAN YOUR AGREEMENTS FIELD

Since the early 2000s, my group at the Institute for Strategic Clarity has been working with agreements with groups across the globe. This work has expanded through a network of colleagues, friends and groups engaging their networks, their companies, their teams, and individuals in their own lives. In all these thousands of groups, across all these countries, a pattern emerged. Your assumptions, agreements, interactions, experiences, and outcomes are all happening at the same time.

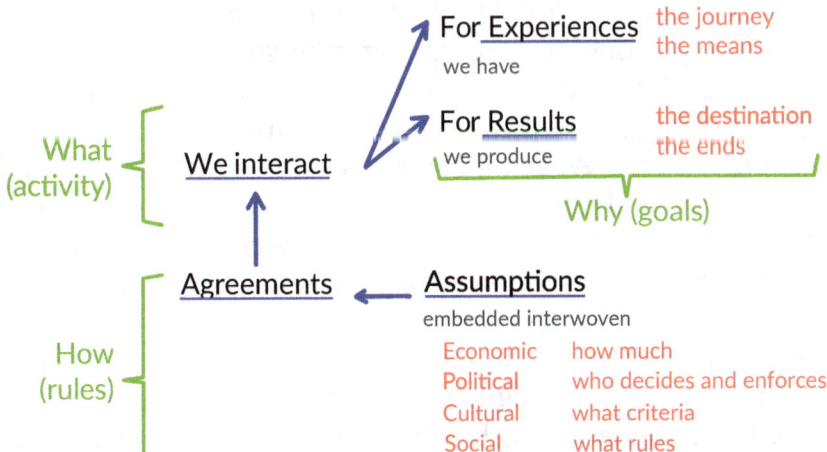

For **Experiences** the journey
we have the means

For **Results** the destination
we produce the ends

We interact

What
(activity)

Why (goals)

Agreements ← **Assumptions**
embedded interwoven

How
(rules)

Economic how much
Political who decides and enforces
Cultural what criteria
Social what rules

Figure 4: Your Agreements Field

How do we want to try to understand what we are seeing? No single framework seemed to explain very much. It was not simply a cultural question. Or a systems problem. Or a strategic decision-making frame. In looking for people who were describing similar things, we started to combine ideas from physics, chemistry, biology, psychology, decision sciences, economics, political science, cultural anthropology, and sociology. We started to see that we were describing a field.

By a field, we mean that it is one essence, one thing, one energy. As you move around in this field, you can measure certain aspects, and it changes. Like with a magnetic field. You have probably seen the pictures of the patterns the iron filings create around the magnet. If you have not, look for the images online. The iron filings form patterns around the magnet. The magnet is the thing itself, and there is an energy field around it, which you can indirectly see by the patterns. People discovered that electricity does the same thing, that there's an electrical field, which led to Maxwell's famous electromagnetic field equations in the late 1800s. Albert Einstein is famous for a field-theory description of general relativity. People began to realize that these things they observe are fields. Fields of energy. Mass as fields of energy.

Going back to your experience, connecting these dots, what if all of this is happening at the same time? Your assumptions, the agreements around your interactions, experiences, and outcomes. All in one agreements field. What if you move through the day, and through your life, through different sets of agreements? We explored this in the previous chapter. How do you know when you are in an agreement? You always are. What is that agreement moving towards? What is that purposeful energy? What are the differences in those experiences? We talked of harmonics, in the vibrancy experienced, in the power, the abundance. Maybe the question is, "What agreements field are you in?"

As I was beginning to bring insights from these many disciplines together to describe agreements fields, a colleague of the CHOICE Foundations Lab wondered whether we could use the agreements field to look at what groups can do, as compared to what they say they can do. Do different agreements fields have different capacities? How would we know?

We started to describe the agreements and capacities we observed in groups we had supported. As it is the focus of this colleague's work, we started with the capacity for systems thinking in collaborative networks. While many groups say they are collaborative networks for systems change, we knew from experience that what they said, what they meant, and what they could do were often very different things. Chapter 1 explored this briefly, seeing that your group might say that it is really good at developing new capacities, but when you look at the group's actual actions, you see that they are not good at that.

How would they know the difference between what a group says it can do and what it is capable of doing? You have what it says, its brochure or website, and then there is what it is doing. What is really happening in its interactions is a function of its underlying agreements. The assumptions they actually have, around the agreements of their interactions, experiences and outcomes, versus their words.

We realized that we could measure this, and that this measurement allows us to differentiate levels of an agreements field. There is a continuum, from very basic, extractive groups to learning, cooperative groups to collaborative high-performing groups to deeply collaborative ecologies of sacred hospitality.

Along this continuum, we started to realize that these groups had very different demonstrated capacities for four things which were interesting to us. My colleague asked about their capacity for understanding systems. A lot of people say they are *systems thinkers*. What does systems thinking look like along this continuum of the agreements field? In describing many groups we had worked with, we started to see a continuum of what systems thinking might mean, from focusing only on outcomes of the system, at the very basic level, to thinking about the dynamics of learning and outcomes at the cooperative level, to thinking about the dynamics of achieving a deeper shared purpose at the collaborative level, to sacred hospitality at the deep collaboration level. Very different understandings of what a group can do, and what it means to think systemically.

We looked at the behavior of hundreds of groups that we knew and had worked with. We observed what they had demonstrated they could do when they said systems thinking. We also did the same around *collaborative capacity*. What does it mean to say that you have collaborative capacity, at these different levels? Does it look different? Indeed, it did. We saw that collaborative capacity varied by what the group means by collaborative capacity, and by the underlying assumptions the group has about the world. How they interact, the experiences they have, the outcomes they achieve, and their impact. We found that these all have very different expressions of what collaborative capacity means at these different levels.

We then explored *added value*. What is the added value of the group's work? What does the group mean by the value that they generate? This continuum showed up again, with very different expressions from very extractive, to trying to see that everyone gets what they need, to generating positive value, to seeing that the total value generated throughout the ecosystem is far greater because of their interactions. The added value is different along the continuum.

We then looked at *network readiness*. How ready is the group to work as a network? Do we have the capacities and structures in place to be able to work as a network? As is starting to become obvious, we found a continuum. Some people are only paying attention to themselves, to their own outcomes and capacities. Some are also paying attention to others and their capacities, as well as their own capacities. Some are also paying attention to what the group is trying to achieve, as well as the capacities of the other and their own capacities, in how they interrelate with each other and developing over time and outcomes the group can achieve. Those are very different levels of network readiness.

We described what we were seeing and experiencing across a wide variety of networks. Along this continuum, the groups demonstrated very different levels of agreements and network readiness. This led us to realize that these four things that we were asking—systemic understanding, collaborative capacity, added value, and network readiness—were highly correlated. From an agreements-field perspective, that is not surprising. Or, it should be less surprising, because in each of these four things, the groups are starting from the same basic assumptions. The low levels of these four things are the results of groups starting with lower assumptions and agreements. They started with the assumptions of separation, of scarcity, of a No!

The higher up we moved on the continuum of agreements, the more the group aligned their assumptions, interactions, experiences, and outcomes with their Yes! We started to see that what the group means by systemic understanding, collaborative capacity, added value, and network readiness changes consistently as they move through the continuum of agreements.

Putting these four terms together, we came up with the acronym SCAN, with the S for systemic understanding, the C for collaborative capacity, the A for added value, and the N for network readiness. Your SCAN allows you to see the strength of your agreements field, and what you mean by systemic understanding, collaborative capacity, added value, and network readiness. Some people think of this as due diligence, confirming what is happening.

The Institute for Strategic Clarity developed the SCAN to be able to see, with the group, what they mean when they say they are doing systemic change in a collaborative way with a network. What they mean versus what they say, whether the capacities that they are demonstrating can do this.

We took a framework that we had been developing for describing agreements fields and used it to assess where a group is on the continuum. With this framework, they could get a sense of where they stand, what that means for what they are capable of now, and what they can shift to be able to do what is being required of them. As well as what they need to shift to be able to have greater systemic understanding, collaborative capacity, added value, and network readiness. So, where are they? What are they capable of? Are they able and ready to shift to a higher level of agreements?

Now we have moved from what you say you can do to assessing the level of where you are in your capacity along a continuum. What are the dimensions of this agreements field that we are measuring in the SCAN?

DIMENSIONS OF AGREEMENTS FIELDS

We have developed the initial mathematics for describing an agreements field. What does that mean to you? It means we have the dimensions of the agreements field. We have formulas for these dimensions. We have the geometry of how these dimensions fit together. We have a mathematical, geometric interpretation of what this means.

We have developed tools and practices for assessing each of these dimensions in a quick diagnostic. With a deeper, evidence-based diagnostic, we can validate more robustly and rigorously each of these dimensions, validating them with evidence of what the group is doing. We can use the group's reported measures and its internal beliefs about its measures. We can validate with the group their understanding of where they are. This brings rigor and robustness to validate that this is what is happening. Taking on the mathematics and geometries can be a bit much. For now, what might be more useful is to have an intuitive sense of the dimensions of an agreements field. Your agreements field. Describing what you are experiencing in an agreements field, when you know that you are in one. Which you always are.

Because the agreements field has energy that is moving toward something, it has some purpose embedded in it. How do you understand that, so you can see the assumptions around the agreements of your interactions, experiences, and outcomes all together, at the same time? Seeing this gives you the power to see what you can shift, so that you can choose your agreements.

Overview

Let us try to build an intuitive understanding of these dimensions, this dimensionality of this agreements field, as one agreements field. This will allow you to better understand and choose your agreements. We can think of this from three different perspectives: engaging, transforming, and transferring.

This agreements field is an energetic field. Like in the magnetic field and the electrical field. Something is flowing through this field. With the agreements field, you are looking at how you engage with that energy. When you bring together an agreements field, you are trying to organize around a principle. In the schools of business administration, public administration, and public health, where I have been teaching since the early 1990s, you are looking at the principle around which you organize. The organizing principle. This principle focuses on connecting people to the energy of something you are trying to do. With that energy, you are trying to transform something. Transforming energy into something for someone, a product or a service. Giving someone access to something. You add value by doing something that others appreciate. Something others want to be in relationship with. Or to receive. To do that, people have to engage.

The first part of thinking about this agreements field is about how to engage that energy. How you engage that purposeful energy that you want to use to do something. Then you want to know how to transform the energy that you have engaged. How good are you at transforming the energy you have engaged? Are you transforming it in a way that others want? Can you transfer that to others? Do they want it? Can they engage with it, and can they engage with it in the form that you are offering it?

You can think of this agreements field as your ability to engage, to plug into the source of energy, to transform it into something else, and then to let it flow out of your system towards others in a way that resonates with what they want and are able to receive – engaging, transforming, and transferring. These are the three keys to unlocking the potential that is in your agreements field (see Figure 5). These three keys enable you to move from where you are to a higher level of agreements, from accepting a No! to choosing your Yes!

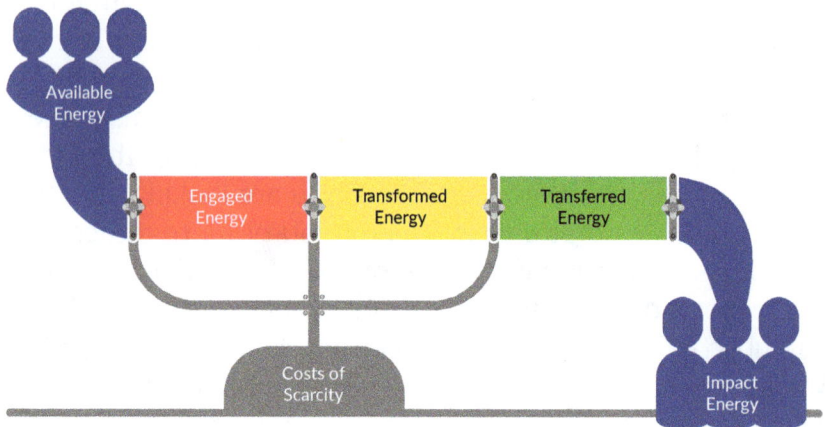

Figure 5: 3 Keys to Unlock Potential in Your Agreements Field

Now we can dig in a little bit. What are the dimensions within each of these three components of your agreements field: engaging, transforming and transferring?

Engaging

In the engaging dimensions of your agreements field, you are plugging into the motivating force, into the purposeful energy. What is the purpose for why you are doing this, why you are connecting? The first question looks at whether you are actually plugged in. To get the energy to flow, like with your desk lamp, you have to plug it into the energy source.

Connected to Purpose
In the previous chapter, you saw that you prefer the experience of agreements that have more harmonic, more vibrancy, more power, more abundance. So how do you get it? It has to be plugged in. Plugged into what? Into that purposeful energy. The first question that we ask about engaging is what

percentage of the time are you plugged in? Do you remember what your purpose is? Is it present in this moment? When you are making decisions? Or do you have the experience of saying Yes! to some purpose, but you do not even remember what it is? Maybe it is written down somewhere. Right now, you are not actually talking about that. If you were to look around the room, at all the others in the room with you, at any given moment, would you even know what they are talking about? Would you know exactly what the purpose is that drives what they are trying to do in that moment? What they are organizing their thinking and acting around? Are they conscious and clear on their motivating purpose? Or do they all have different perceptions in the room of what that purpose is?

Informal Survey. I often ask, as an informal survey, right now, in this moment, what do you think we are working on? What are we working towards? What is the principle that is organizing us? What is our goal? What is our purpose, right now? If you feel safe in the group, try asking this yourself. I find that most people think, in most meetings they are in, that they are working on different things. They are not actually working towards the same purpose.

I even find these days that many people do not know why they are in the meeting, other than that someone put the meeting in their calendar. Many discover they are in the wrong meeting, but say nothing about it, to not disturb others.

Many people are talking these days about the purpose-driven organization, the purpose-led team, or purpose in your life. While it is not new, it is not widely practiced, not on a continuous basis, and at great cost. The question here is about being plugged in. Are you connected to the purpose, and is it motivating what you are doing? Is it guiding your questions? Are you working towards something consciously? What percentage of the time are you connected to that, now?

Unique Diversity
If you are connected, then the second dimension of engaging focuses on what is coming in. What are you seeing in the group, in the circle of people that are sitting with you? What

is coming in? Do you need the perspective of the different voices of who is in the room? What they can see and observe as it is coming in, as you are connecting to the purpose?

When groups have very weak agreements fields, when they are starting with a No!, you experience that there is less harmonic, less vibrancy, less power, less abundance in these groups and typically you find one person talking at the others.

Informal Survey. In another informal survey, I ask people how many ideas they have had in the last hour, sitting in that meeting, in that room. I ask them to write that down. Typically, they tell me they have had 10-15 ideas. Then I ask them how many they shared. Often they tell me they shared none or maybe one. Then I ask them why they did not share the other 9-14 ideas they had. Invariably they say, because they were not asked. There was not any space for them to share their ideas. Nobody was listening. And they observe that it does not make any difference when they do share.

This is the experience in the lower levels of the agreements field. In the weaker agreements, where there is less harmonic, less vibrancy, less power, and less abundance. The experience that you prefer less.

In contrast, when groups with strong agreement fields connect to the purpose, everyone is sharing what they are learning. They all know that they need each other to share what they are seeing, because they are different. This is the reason they are in this room, in the first place. They each see the world differently. They know how each other sees the world differently, and they hold each other to the standard of bringing their best game, exactly because each one sees the world differently.

A brief example. I was in a conversation a couple of years ago where the company was trying to decide whether it could make money selling a specific product. They knew that the customers loved the product, and that their company was really good at making it. The question was whether they could make money making the product, as a company. For this exploration, they put three people in the room with me. The engineer in charge of making it. The marketing person selling it. And the accountant who understood how the company's finances worked. With these three people, we could answer the question of how much they could make selling this. The marketing person said, "If it has these characteristics, this is what I believe people will pay for it, and this is the volume of sales that we could have." The engineer said, "This is what it will cost to make the product, in time and resources." They then turned to the accountant, who said that given these revenues (the inflows) and given those costs (the outflows), and given the infrastructure needed to be able to do that, and given their overhead, then, yes, they could profitably make and sell this product at that volume, price, and cost. "We can make enough money to be able to support ourselves in continuously doing this, while reinvesting in ourselves."

In this example, you clearly need each of the three perspectives. What would happen if one of the three did not give their input? What if the process was like the one we described above for the weak agreements field? Where the people in the room shared only one in ten of their ideas? Where they are not listening for the perspectives of the others? Where they are not listening for the perspectives required? In that room they do not know that they need each other, that they need to know what the other is thinking. When they were clear that the question was whether the business could be successful producing and selling this product, it required all three perspectives. How much is it going to cost? How much can they sell it for? Can they make a profit, so that they can support themselves and reinvest going forward? They need all three of those perspectives. They realize that they need all three. They can hold each other to a high level of performance of what excellence looks like for each of them, and what they brought. In that case, can you imagine one of them saying that they do not feel like talking today? It was a three-part question that required three perspectives. Each perspective is different. This requires participating. This is the second part of engaging.

Trust

The third dimension is the experience that you have, the trust you experience. You have connected to the purpose. You have the right perspectives in the room. You know how to listen to those perspectives. Do you trust that you can share, and to what level?

Usually we see that groups come from very low agreements, where people only focus on outcomes. So, don't talk about that learning and that possibility stuff. Just tell me what you already know. That is in the No!, in the net negative.

From your own experiences, you have most probably experienced this, as well as the other end of that continuum, where you trust that you can share what you know from the past, as well as what you are seeing now and starting to learn, towards the future.

Going back to the example of the three people trying to decide whether they could profitably make and sell a product. From their previous experience selling these types of products, they knew they could sell it at a specific price point. That is what they knew from the already finished, what already happened. And they could also try a couple of things to confirm what they observed before, and maybe also learn something new. They could try a small, low-risk experiment with a pilot test. They could pilot test how they would make it, and they could pilot test how they would sell it, trying this and that. The accountant saw that they had the resources to try and how they could measure what they might learn. This is the becoming, the developing of new capacities and relationships, learning.

Taking it to the next level, the level of possibility, of potential, they saw that they had seen a future possibility of a new way of producing and selling this product. That would put them in experimentation mode. They could then see what they learned along the way, towards the possible outcome they saw together, get the feedback, and then adjust what they saw in the possibility and in the pathway to a new outcome. They would be evolving.

Moving to each of these new levels of work opens up and engages whole new levels of energy, in each individual and in the group. It is more creative, more exciting, more engaging. Moving to each new level also requires trust. Trust that you can share new, uncertain ideas into the group. This is when you ask yourself, "How much of what I can see do I trust to share into the room? Only what I already know for certain? Or also what I am starting to learn? Or maybe even what I see in potential?"

As seen in the previous chapter, you observe, from your own experience, that you prefer agreements where there is a greater harmonic, greater vibrancy, greater power, and great abundance. We can now start to describe the structure of what is happening in that experience. You are engaging, transforming, and transferring.

Dimensions of Engaging Your Agreements Field
1. Purpose-driven
2. Unique diversity
3. Trust

You are connecting to a purpose, and to the energy that connection brings. The energy comes in through the different perspectives in the group. Are you each listening for what is coming in, through each person's perspective, requiring that each other share what is being perceived? Is there enough trust in the room that you are sharing what you already know, and what you are learning, and the potential that you are seeing? This whole first perspective of engaging is about being connected, plugged in, having the right voices in the room, knowing how to listen and inquire so that each person brings in their unique perspectives, and trusting enough to share what they already know, what they are starting to learn, and what they might be able to see, their potential. These are three engaging elements.

Transforming

After engaging, the second part focuses on transforming the energy into something else. Do we know how to transform that energy? An intuitive way of thinking about this is that you plugged in, so the energy is now flowing. Now you have to connect the group's social structure to that energy inflow. Does the group know how to work with the energy that is given? Do they know how to transform that engaged energy? How good are they at transforming what they received? Do they have access to the resources on a resilient basis, so that they can be continuously transforming?

Ecosystem Infrastructure
Diving into a little more nuance, the first dimension of transforming asks if the group is set up to be able to work with the different levels of energy inflow. Do the group structures and processes only ask about and only pay attention to what is already known?

Or do they also have structures and processes in place that work with learning? They ask, "Is it what you said this last week? You said you were going to go try this last week. You learned something. What was it that you learned? How does that affect what we already knew? How does that affect our processes and structures procedures going forward?" At this level, the group is set up to be able to change over time.

Or is the group structured to be able to also look into its potential? "You said that is what we knew yesterday, and that we were trying something new. What is it that we need to be paying attention to? How do we change how we are constituted, so that we can continuously be improving? So that we are continuously getting better outcomes?" This has to do with the system that plugs into that engaging energy. Is the group able to work at the outcomes-only level, or the outcomes and learning levels, or the outcomes and learning and potential levels?

Systemic Leverage
The second dimension in transforming is around knowing what to do with that energy once it comes in. The engaged

energy is an input, along with the other resources needed to provide this product or service. This dimension focuses on the level of efficiency and effectiveness the group has in leveraging that energy, transforming it into something else. This leverage happens systemically, at three very basic levels.

The first level of leverage is in *direct action*. The capacity to know what to do, specifically, with each one of those inputs. How efficient are the specific actions taken? How much experience and knowledge goes into the design of these specific actions? Are they very efficient, meaning that they get a big bang for the buck? Or is it that they do not really understand what they are doing. Like me in the kitchen, they do not know how to cut an onion efficiently, so it takes me five minutes to cut the onion. A professional chef can prepare that same onion in seconds, much more cleanly, much more exactly, and much more safely. So, there are differences in how efficient a group can be in transforming inputs directly into something else.

The second level of leverage is in the feedback loops within the system. This focuses on the group's understanding of the *dynamics* of how things work within the system. Do they understand the system's dynamics or are they fighting them? The system embodies dynamics that help maintain the level that it is at right now. Like the homeostatic nature of the thermostat in your house. This balancing mechanism stabilizes the system at a specific level of performance. The system also has dynamics that escalate or move very quickly. When the group understands the basic system dynamics of their work, they work with the dynamics of their system, not against them. For example, when a group works with the river, it takes very little effort to access, engage, and leverage the huge force in the flow of the river. Working against the river requires putting in a great amount of energy and getting only a small amount out.

The third level of leverage coordinates the system dynamics within different areas of the system. You are working with the wind and the river. You are working with the systemic conditions, within each of the areas, bringing them together, as the *structure* of the system coordinating the focus on reinforcing feedback with balancing feedback to grow and sustain, toge-ther as a system. These are the three levels of leverage: direct; dynamic; and structural.

What does working with a wide range of groups over the past decades show? Groups with weak agreements fields are usually weak at all three, lacking ecosystem structures to frame, understand, and act with systemic leverage. Groups with moderate agreements fields are usually strong in the efficiency of their direct actions, experienced in their dynamics, and working on the coordination of their structural leverage. Groups with strong agreements collaboratively evolve all three levels of leverage continuously and coherently.

Resilience

The third transforming dimension focuses on resilience. Do you have structures that give you access to the resources the system needs? These are like the roots and branches of the tree that reach out for nutrients, water, sun, and air. Do you have the structures that can access these resources on a continuous basis? How resilient are they?

Groups with weak agreements fields are always begging and always scrounging for resources. They spend a lot of energy trying to get any resources they can. Groups with moderate agreements fields have access to one key source or a couple of resources, but that access is contingent on the decisions of those sources. More regenerative groups, with strong agreements fields, have access to multiple resources and flexibility of their structures of access to be able to get those resources from multiple places. They usually generate some of the resources on their own. They can generate the resources that they need themselves, so that they are not contingent on the short-term decisions of another group. What is the resilience of that access?

Dimensions of Transforming Your Agreements Field
1. Ecosystem infrastructure
2. Systemic leverage
3. Resilience

You now have three transformation dimensions. When you plug into that engaged energy, how much of that energy are you getting? Do you know how to use that energy to transform it directly, dynamically, and structurally into something else that drives values for others? Do you have access, on a continuous, resilient basis to the resources you need?

Transferring

In addition to engaging the energy and transforming it, the agreements field also transfers that transformed energy to someone else. This transfer has two dimensions.

Connecting with Intended Recipient

The basic question of the first dimension is whether the intended recipients of the transformed energy want it and are able to receive it in the form that you are offering it. Are you offering them soup when what they need is clothes? Are you offering them services when what they need is the result? This calls to mind the famous example of trying to sell the drill when what the client wants is the hole in the wall. Do they want the hole, or do they want the drill? How do you know? How are you engaging them? Are you listening to them?

In transferring the energy, there is also a continuum, from groups that do this at very low levels to groups that transfer energy at very high levels. While groups at different places on this continuum have very different practices, groups at similar places on the continuum have practices based on similar agreements.

When I ask people if they know how much money they are making, in this moment, most can tell me to the penny how much they are making. Whether it is an individual or the leaders of a large organization, they know. They have the systems in place to be able to know that. Precisely and now.

Then I ask them how the recipients of their work are evolving in what they want. They usually tell me that they occasionally survey their recipients. Maybe every couple of years. This means that they are not in touch. They are not actively connected to the intended recipients. Even when they have people in their organization who talk to the intended recipient every day, the leaders rarely get their input. Many organizations now even outsource the contact with the intended recipients to a different company in a different country—often a very low-cost, customer-engagement service. They do not know. This is how most organizations are on the low end of the continuum. On the high end of the continuum, the recipient of what you are doing is deeply involved, all the time. You are co-designing the experience they are having, with them, so you know exactly what they want. They are designing it with you. The transformed energy is transferred to them, the intended recipients.

Inclusion

The second dimension of transferring energy asks who is the intended recipient of your engaged and transformed energy? Is your system serving everybody everywhere in that system every day? What percentage of the people that you say you are serving can receive it, and actually do receive it, in the form that you are offering it? Is it serving everyone in your system, everywhere in your system, every day? This is called E^3, pronounced eCubed. The next chapter will describe E^3 in more depth.

You now have two parts of the ability to transfer the transformed energy. What it is you are transferring. Whether the intended recipients want it and can receive it in the form offered. And the percentage of the intended recipients actually being served.

Dimensions of Transferring Your Agreements Field

1. Connecting with intended recipient
2. Inclusion

Coming full circle, your agreements are in an agreements field, which contains underlying assumptions, interactions, experiences, and outcomes, all together. In your agreements, you are connecting to the purposeful energy, the energy that is always there, that is always transforming to something else. How well are you connecting to that available energy? How well are you transforming that engaged energy into something you can transfer to someone who wants it and can receive it in the form you are offering? In this one agreements field, you are engaging, transforming, and transferring energy. These three different ways of understanding this one agreements field give you three different ways of unlocking the potential within your agreements field.

ONE AGREEMENTS FIELD

In the next chapter, you will see that you cannot work on just one of these three areas of engaging, transforming, or transferring at a time. You cannot say that you are just going to work on engaging and not on transforming and transferring. If you do, you still lose all the energy. The key insight is that it is one agreements field. You can work on different dimensions, knowing that you are changing all of them.

The Institute for Strategic Clarity's global survey and fieldwork has found ways that people are discovering to work on how they engage, transform, and transfer their purposeful energy, their creativity, all at the same time. This is contingent on a very simple set of assumptions, which we will be getting into later in the book. The main point, for now, is that it is one agreements field that engages the energy, transforms it, and transfers it.

Remembering that the underlying assumptions, interactions, experiences, and outcomes are all in the same moment provides the entry point for working on the engaging, transforming, and transferring elements of the agreements field all at the same time. What are the underlying assumptions that you have that enable your agreements field, at the level you have right now? What level can you achieve if you step further into your Yes!?

If you have a weak agreements field, you are focused purely on the outcomes. This focus means that you engage, transform, and transfer from an outcomes-only focus. If you have a strong agreements field, you are focused on possibilities and developing and outcomes.

This understanding of the level of your agreements field also tells you about key capacities your agreements field has and what it can produce. Lots of organizations these days talk about facing challenging issues by coming from a systemic perspective, using collaborative networks to drive deep impact. Having observed hundreds and hundreds of groups now, in dozens of countries, the level of their agreements field correlates highly with their level of systemic understanding, collaborative capacity, added value, and network readiness. The agreements field level allows you to know what a group means when they say they have the capacities of systemic understanding, collaboration, added value, and network readiness. It means something very specific when they have a weak agreements field, and it means something very different when they have a medium-or high-level agreements field.

The Institute for Strategic Clarity's research, has begun to discover what those practices look like. Now we can start to say, with the SCAN of your agreements field, where you are versus where your brochure says you are, and what that means for the capacities you have, right now. You can then decide what capacities you need to have to do what you know is yours to do. Your Yes! To know the capacities in your agreements field that you require, and what those practices look like. This allows you to assess whether you are up to making the required shifts in your agreements field. You can see whether you are ready to start moving in that direction. In the next chapter, you will start to look at what it means to step into this.

AGREEMENTS FIELDS WHERE E^3=100%

AN INTUITIVE FEEL

Returning to the question of your agreements field. What do you intend to do with this purposeful energy? Why are you engaging it, transforming it, and transferring it? To whom? For what purpose? One of the ways that seems intuitive to work with these questions is to reflect on who it is affecting and how well it is doing that. What is the desired agreements field that you have versus the actual one you have? What are you trying to serve? To what level of purpose, of goal, of objectives? What does that impact look like? What are you doing? One way of thinking about that is what called E^3 (pronounced eCubed). E_1 times E_2 times E_3. E_1 is everyone. E_2 is everywhere. E_3 is every day. Everyone everywhere everyday.

Everyone, as it extends out over space, and every day as it extends over time. Everyone everywhere everyday. So, let's look at your desired system. Whoever you say that you are trying to serve. Whatever the purpose is for what you are trying to generate. Whether it is making a fun family dinner or inviting friends over for the weekend. Whether it is profitability for your company, getting people out of poverty, or fighting disease. Whatever it is that you are doing. Who is it intended for? To what level?

You have some goal. Is it intended for everyone? Who is this everyone that it is intended for? Is it intended for the people in your neighborhood only? Is it intended for some of the people in your neighborhood? Is it intended for everybody in your town?

For example, what about the kids in our public school system? That includes all the kids that are attending public school, kindergarten through 12th grade, in the geographic confines of our city. That would be a definition of everyone everywhere everyday. That means that it works in all different demographics. If it does not, does it work particularly well in poorer communities or in richer communities? Does it work better in different ethnic communities? Does it work better for different genders? Is it better for different ages? Who and what is it intended for?

It is intended for everyone, in all the different demographics of your system. It matters how you define what those demographics are. They say it is public school for all kids. That means all ethnic groups, genders, sexual orientations, ages. It is intended for all children in that age group.

You define E^3 when you set up the agreements field. Now you are asking what is that that you are intending to do? When you define the system, your desired agreements field, you define it as everyone everywhere everyday. Therefore, the everyone (E_1) times everywhere (E_2) times every day (E_3). E_1 times E_2 times E_3 equals 100%.

You get all the people, in all of the demographies that you have stated, all of the time that you have stated. E^3 for your system is 100%. With that, what is the actual agreements field? What percentage of the people are you getting to? What percentage of the demographies are you getting to? What percentage of the time are you getting to them?

This does not mean that you must get to all of the people, everywhere, all of the time. You are getting to all the people that you said your system was designed to reach. In setting your purpose, your mission, you identified an agreements field that is intended for everywhere within that system that you said, all the time that you said. How well are you actually doing that? Less gives you an E^3 that is less than 100%.

A public school system that should be 100% was actually 52%. Half of the kids are met some of the time. This is far less than the 100% they said that it should be. You can think of this in two ways: (1) the E^3 is for the desired level; or (2) E^3 is for what you are doing. The first way shows that half of the kids are met with the system that was designed for all of the kids. Or, seen the second way, the system is E^3 = 100%. The current system is meeting all of the kids, in all of the geographies, all of the time that it was actually designed for. In this case, E^3 = 100%, meaning it is doing what it was designed to do, which might be different than its stated purpose.

This understanding highlights who the system was designed for. That then lets you see whether you intended it to be for another group than the one that it is serving now. This assessment brings clarity on the gap between who you are serving and who you desire to serve with the system. This gap sets you up for coming back to your Yes! Is it okay where you are? Are you doing what you actually set out to do, independent of what was on your brochure? Are you okay with what you are actually doing? If not, then you can redefine this. The people that you were intending to serve can be the people that you are serving. That is different than pretending you desire to be serving other people than those you are serving. This aligns you with your big Yes! Let's look at a few examples of E^3 in projects we have been involved with over the last few years.

EXAMPLES OF E^3

Back in the early 1990s, I was an advisor to the Secretary of Health in Mexico on the epidemiology of dengue. The stated E^3 was no Mexicans were to get infected, sick, or die. We knew the fact that whenever dengue came into the country, there was an outbreak. The public health system in place had demonstrated that it was not able to keep Mexicans from getting dengue. It was not able to stop the outbreak. The actual E^3 was far lower than 100%. Who did this actual system serve? Who should it serve?

We said everyone, everywhere, everyday, E^3=100%, for all Mexicans. This required a different system and agreements field.

You can see a similar thing in kindergarten through 12th grade public education in the state of Massachusetts. Massachusetts is ranked in the United States as one of the better states in public, primary and secondary education. The state's public education system has lots of resources and money, with well-qualified teachers, lots of experience, lots of initiatives serving the children in the state. So, then the question is, how well is the system doing at achieving that? If we look at that from the standard of the state exam, as one measure of success of the kindergarten to 12th grade public system, when we were doing this initiative in 2017, 52% of the children graduating high school in the state of Massachusetts, through the public K-12 system, were scoring proficient or better on the MCAS, the state exam. So, 52%. According to this measure, 52% were being met by the system. The other 48% were not. What became obvious to most of the folks working in the system was that it was predictable, by geography, where it was not. So, the system, as scored on this state exam, showed that it was able to meet some of the kids in some of the places some of the time. It did not meet all the kids. It never met all the kids in all the places all of the time. Even the kids that it did meet, that scored proficient or better on the state exam, were not met all the time. This is a well-resourced, high-ranking system. This leads to the question, what would they like this E^3 score to be? As they worked through this conversation to get from 52% to something better, the question of how much better was initially very difficult. From 52%, can they get to 70%? Can they get to 80%? Given all the efforts and all of the resources that are being put into this, in the state, now and in the last two decades? With the E^3 concept, the question flipped, and became obvious and easy. Who is the system intended to serve? It was very clear to everyone in the power structure of the system, in the room with us. The K-12 public education system in the state of Massachusetts is here to serve all children within the state, all the time. The public school system. Therefore, E^3 must equal 100%.

Another large-scale initiative we were involved with, 2009-2010 and periodically since, was around the energy future of the state of Vermont (USA). The goal that the group put before itself was taking on collaboratively a systemic issue within the state. Its energy future was a key issue that they decided to focus on, bringing together leadership across the state. It became clear that none of the energy for Vermont was generated within Vermont. Not for heating, which is critical during the long New England winters, and not for electricity or transportation. All the energy came from outside of the state. A core Vermont value is sovereignty in decision-making. Vermonters making decisions for Vermonters. They needed to be able to control all their energy future. Energy price swings, up or down—at this time the price of oil was going up—had a severe impact on the economic livelihood of many Vermonters. Since Vermont did not control the source of any energy, all coming from outside the state, they decided they wanted to have sovereignty over 100% of their energy future. When they started the project, they controlled 0%. How could they reach 100% control? That exploration led the focus to renewable energies, not because everybody in the state was very strongly for renewable energy, rather that was the way that they could provide for their heating, electricity, and transportation, from completely within the state. They were able to converge on that audacious shift because of Vermont's core value of sovereignty. So, if E^3 means energy future for all Vermonters everywhere in Vermont, poor and rich, north, and south of the state, all the time, what does a solution look like? Right now, $E^3 = 0\%$, and it needs to be $E^3 = 100\%$. What do they need to do? What would that world look like? How do they shift towards it?

YOUR GROUP

Now, let's go to your group. What is your E^3? What is the measure that you have for the success of what you are trying to do? How successful are you at that, for the people that you are serving? Whether it is your friends at a dinner party, your own family, yourself, your business, or whatever group you are serving. What percentage of the people do you reach? Does it reach everybody that it is intended to reach, in all geographies?

All demographies? Does it reach them all the time that you say that you want to? What is the E^3 of your actual system? What does that actual E^3 tell you about that 100%? Where you are, compared to your desired state. Who are you serving? Is that good enough for you? Does that align with your big Yes!? Or is there another Yes! there? You must see how you are going to shift your system to be able to serve them.

THE 9 CHOICES YOU HAVE IN YOUR AGREEMENTS FIELD

You have many choices in your agreements field. Your Yes! How you engage, transform, and transfer purposeful energy. What are the specific choices you have?

YOUR YES!

Going back to where we started, we observed that the initial conditions you start with determine whether you are saying Yes! or No! This leads to a net-positive or net-negative impact. If you say Yes!, no matter how poorly you do that, how much you forget, you are aligned with your Yes! The result you observe is always net positive. You generate more value than you extract from the system.

When you start with No!, or you accept the No! somewhere in your agreements, the results are always net negative. You generate less value than you extract from the system.

We started to look at what agreements are. How you know when you are in an agreement. What you can do about it. That there are agreements fields. What some of the dimensions are. We now want to look at what your choices are.

What Purposeful Energy Is

What are your choices in an agreements field? We start with purposeful energy. In the beginning of this exploration into your Yes!, we started with the observation from physics, chemistry, and biology that everything in this universe—what we call the universe—is energy. All matter is energy, as Einstein so elegantly showed us. Mass equals energy. Add in a relationship to the speed of light. It is literally this massive relationship between mass and energy. Everything is energy. We said energy moves from one form to another, it trans-forms, by definition. In moving from one form to another, it is moving toward something.

For social purposes, for social interactions, we want to know what is moving. What is this purpose that it is moving towards? Can you define it? Can you work with it? This is one of your first and most powerful leverage points for choices in your agreements field. What is the purpose that you are in service to? What is it that you know that you are here to do? To contribute to, within any of the systems that you are in. Whether it is your intimate relationships, your own personal health, your children, friends, parents, work, friends, church, sport. Whatever it is that you are doing. What is it that you are trying to achieve?

How You Know

How do you know that? One of the ways that you know that it is your calling is your pull. Something that gets your attention. Something that pulls you towards it. It gets your excitement. Your energy. What is this? What is this, and why do you feel called to it? Other, deeper questions lie within your own cosmovision of the calling. Who determines your calling? What determines it? Is it determined in previous lives or now? However you choose to see it. But what you can know is whether you are responding to the purpose that is yours to serve, within this setting. Whatever that setting is, are you aligned with it? Are you fighting it? The first question that you can start to ask is, what is the purpose here? Does it make sense to you? Do you understand what it is? Is it something that you agree to?

For example, what is the purpose for those working in public-school education? Is the purpose to get all the kids to be taken care of? Is it daycare for kindergarten through twelfth grade kids, or is it thriving for all children in public education? Is it to pass a state exam? Is it to be better citizens?

What about your purpose in your job? What is it? What is the purpose of what you are doing at work? Your big Yes! at work. Is it to make money for somebody? That could be shareholder value maximization. Is it to serve your customers and provide excellent service? It could be. That could be customer satisfaction. Is it that you have a great place to work, as you do something, and as you make money for the owner's equity? What is that purpose that brings you together?

As we said in the previous chapter, this purpose is the organizing principle. What is it that you are organizing around? If you do not know this, then it is much more difficult to achieve it. So, what is it? What does it mean? How does it help you organize?

Because it is the energy that you are connecting to, that you are engaging in, transforming into something for someone. If you know what that is, it is much more likely that you can be efficient and effective over time, and over space, in doing that. It means, to you, that you can engage with this energy, toward something. This is why you care. This is something that energizes you, that you have a contribution to make to, and for some reason it is something that interests you. It gets your interest. Your intention. Your attention.You care about it.

The first choice you have is to identify what this purpose is. To see if it aligns with what you are interested in. That you can contribute to. What it means in your life, the life of your colleagues and others who you are in service to. This is why you care.

There are specific things that you can do to see whether you are able to achieve this purpose or not. You can look at what this deeper purpose is, and you can start to understand what it is, what it means, and how to serve it, within your big Yes!

CHOICE #1: YOUR YES!

Your YES! The purpose with which you engage, that gets your conscious intention and attention.

Closing the Gap in Your Yes!

Is there a gap between where you are, and what it is you desire to achieve with this purpose? Whether you are trying to serve all the children in the state of Massachusetts or simply the half that are maybe being served now. Or is it that you want to have great fellowship with your friends, and sometimes you are successful at that. Maybe you want to have a deep relationship with your partner or your friend. Whatever it is you are trying to do, you can identify the gap. You can understand how important it is to you to the close that gap. So, you actually care about the gap. You want to know what the gap is, so that you can see how important it is to you to close it, how much effort it will take to close it, and whether you are up to the effort, if it is that important to you to shift. If it is your Yes!

The first choice with your purpose is recognizing that purposeful energy exists, and that there is a purpose associated with it. You can identify that purpose, and how you align with it. Identifying the purpose is a choice. Shockingly, most people do not know what these choices are.

Informal Survey. Here's another informal survey I do all the time. I have asked it to hundreds of groups. Why does this group actually exist? Write it down, before anyone says anything in the group. I gather what they have written, and I start reading what they wrote out loud.

Doing it this way does two things. First, it gets everyone's opinion out. If you let someone start to talk into the room, they will state something that the rest of the room has to respond to, by either agreeing or disagreeing. In behavioral decision theory, this is called the anchoring and adjusting bias. Getting people to write it down first makes each person reflect and state, on paper, what they think it is. This gets you a far better idea of what is understood, and not just political reactions for or against what the first person said. Second, it protects the anonymity of those who are voicing their responses. This also helps you get more accurate responses. Otherwise, people might be embarrassed to admit what they think, or it might make them vulnerable to attacks by someone with a different opinion of the group's purpose. A simple process for getting closer to understanding both what people think, as well as the diversity of perspectives in the room.

I find that usually people are thinking that the group is serving different purposes. If everyone thinks that the group exists for different purposes, then they are all moving in those different directions. They are pulling in those directions. They are pushing in those directions. They are pushing in different directions. It is not a united front. They are not moving in the same direction. That is an inefficient use of your resources, as compared to aligning around what your purpose is.

This is the first choice. What is your purpose, and does it align with my purpose and with what I care to contribute? What I think is important to do in the world. What I think is interesting. What gets my attention. In this space, in this place, with these people.

Why You Care

With this clarity, you can then look at the gap. That there is a choice means there is a gap. A gap between what you are intending to serve, and what you are serving. The purpose that you are working towards, and what you are actually achieving. Now you can see how important it is to you that the gap closes. Is it something that you care about? That you care about a lot or not?

We will find a tool and process, in the process section of the book, to help you get specific about the gap. For now, your focus is on your first choice. The importance of this purpose. Does it fit within your big Yes!

With clarity on your Yes! and on the purposeful energy you are engaging with, let's now look at the other eight choices you have within your agreements field.

3 CHOICES IN ENGAGING ENERGY

You have three choices in how you engage your purposeful energy. They are connecting to purpose, knowing whose perspectives are needed to serve that purpose, and creating an environment of trust where people with those perspectives will share what they perceive.

Connecting to Purpose

Your second choice is in the connection to purpose. Given your purposeful energy, what purpose are you serving? Serving what percentage of the time? Are you connected to this? A choice here is to keep present to the choice. You can do this very quickly. It does not take a lot of time to remember all this. For example, you can remind everyone in the group that you know that they are coming from some other place. You know that they are coming from another meeting, another gathering, some other energetic purpose, and now they are here, all together. They are all in alignment with this purpose. I find that this simple reminder is a gift and always useful. Even if it only takes a few seconds to a few minutes to remember what you are in service to.

I told you about an informal survey I do where I ask people what they think the purpose is for why they are in the room together. The purpose of this group. I ask everybody to write it down, before somebody blurts it out, and then read those purposes out loud. It turns out that a big chunk of the people thought they were in different meetings. Or they thought they were in the room for different purposes for the same group. If what you want is for people to be aligned, clear about the purpose they are trying to serve, so that they are on the same purpose, the second choice you can make is connecting to purpose.

A simple way that a friend of mine does this in his meetings is to remind people when they are coming into the same space together. He asks them to give examples of the purpose that they are serving, such as customer service. Today in our business, tell me a story about a customer experience you have had.

You can do the same if it is a dinner party with your friends. Coming together for dinner, it is lovely to have you here in our home. I look forward to the fellowship that we are going to have. This reminds everyone that the purpose is dinner and fellowship. It helps everyone let go of what they were in service to before and allows them to be in this space together now. Simple and powerful.

When the connection to purpose is low, like it appears to be in many groups much of the time, people get attracted to a different purpose. Not the one that was intended when the group was convened. That there is a different purpose is not necessarily problematic. The difficulty is in shifting purposes without being aware of the shift. You think you are there for one purpose, then someone says something that takes it in a different direction, towards a different purpose. Whether intentional or not, this is a shift. Are you agreeing to the shift, or does the shift just happen?

Awareness of the purpose you are serving becomes important when you realize that all your purposeful energy is now in service to that purpose. Who or what is using your will, your intention, your energy? The observation is that your purposeful energy can only be used in one of three ways. It is being used (1) in service to the purpose to which you consciously agreed, (2) in service to another purpose to which you did not agree, or (3) your ability to connect to a purpose is being shut down, and your energy is in service to self-preservation. All three of these are very big users of your creativity, your purposeful energy, because that is what all your creativity is connecting to, in this moment. When you experience a low connection to purpose, usually you are connecting to someone else's purpose, unintentionally, or you are in self-preservation mode. How do you know if this is happening? You feel very disengaged while it is happening, and you probably experience it as very draining.

What are the costs of low connection to purpose? Both the inability to connect the vast amount of human creative energy available to a specific purpose, as well as the massive cost of disengaging people. Disengaged people are not just along for a free ride. They are deeply in self-preservation mode. This is also called burnout. It literally burns them out. The physical, mental, and social health issues resulting from self-preservation caused by disengagement are huge costs.

What are the benefits of high connection to purpose? Two-fold. First, you get access to the vast amount of human creativity already available in the room, all in service to that purpose. Second, you have none of the costs of low connection. This puts you at a distinct advantage because you are not working with the very taxing costs of not connecting. Said another way, high connection to purpose is a more natural state. It is not a heightened state that only special people can do. It is a normal state. As a human being, a *Homo lumens*, you are designed to be creative and to connect that creativity to a purpose, consciously. That is the normal state. Not being connected to purpose is the abnormal state, a state which you unfortunately experience quite frequently.

Start the time together, gathering everyone into the same purpose. Once the meeting is going, this same friend asks another question. When someone else is talking, and he finds that he cannot see how what they are saying connects to the agreed-on purpose, he inquires. Instead of assuming or stating that they are off-purpose, he asks, "I can't see how what you're talking about is linked to our purpose. I trust that it is. I know you are aligned with our purpose. I just need you to help me see it, so that I can understand how this is helping us serve what we are here to do. That way I can connect the dots. If I don't see it, then I'm not connecting them."

These are ways to remind yourself and others of what the purpose is you are serving. This recognizes that everyone is always shifting from one agreements field to another, from one purpose to another, consciously or unconsciously. Always. They were just driving to get here, to the dinner party, from a previous place. Before you were making lunch, and now you are hanging out and watching a movie. Before you were in a marketing meeting, and now you are in a safety meeting. Different purposes. Different agreements fields. And one of the apparent miracles of being human is that it only takes a few seconds to shift gears, allowing everyone to be full connected to the purpose here and now. Whatever it is you are now doing is something different. There are many artistic and clever ways people have found to do this, to remind each other of why they are coming together. They remind everyone of the purpose they are agreeing to serve, so that they can serve it.

If you start to lose focus, if you start to lose the connection to the purposeful energy, you can be creative in how you reconnect. It turns out to be very easy to forget. Helping to reconnect is a gift. A gift of time, of resource, of connection, of service. This is an efficient use of the available energy in the room. Anything else is a massive waste of that energy.

Whose Perspectives Are Needed for This Purpose

Your third choice, in the second "engaging" element, is knowing why you need everybody else in the room. The O Process helps you do this (see Figure 6).

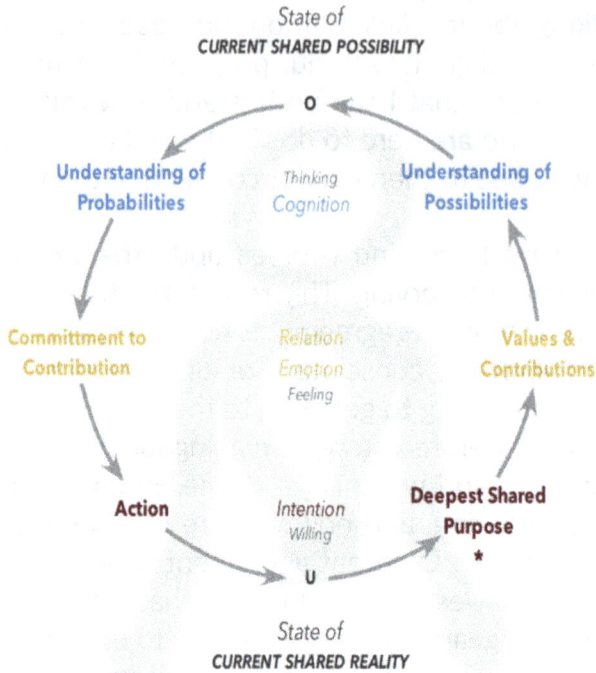

Figure 6: The O Process for Collaborative Alignment

[O Process Narrative—How to read the O Process diagram].
Engaging human beings collaboratively involves aligning their heads, hearts, and hands. The O Process provides a way to do that, aligning within six elements and across them. It starts by connecting to the Deepest Shared Purpose, the intention that brings the group together in the first place. To serve that purpose, you need specific perspectives, each with their own values and contributions. This is where they understand how they relate to the purpose and to each other. You then see what each perspective uniquely sees, in their specific understanding of possibilities. In some moment, those perspectives of possibilities, in service to the deeper shared purpose, come together into the current shared possibility. That is when it can shift into becoming a probability, a reality that each unique perspective can perceive, from their own understanding of what would make that reality probable. Then they can each commit to their unique contributions to manifesting that probability together. This is the flip side of seeing their own values and contributions in possibilities, now contributing

to probabilities. These commitments can now become acts of intention or actions, the use of the will expressed in the deeper shared purpose. Aligning within each step brings everyone to the same deeper connection to purpose. Aligning across each step, aligns the individual and collective willing, feeling, and thinking.

The basic idea is that if you know what you are in service to, what purpose you are serving, you can then clarify whose voices, whose perspectives, you need to have in the room. Let's start with the example I gave in the beginning of the book of trying to decide whether the company can do well making a specific product. Another example was preparing for a dinner party. In the business decision, they need to know whether they can make any money selling this product. That conversation requires the engineer making and costing the product, the marketer selling and pricing the product, and the accountant calculating the sustainable profit. This conversation requires all three perspectives.

Your first two choices were clarity of purpose and connecting to that purpose. The choice now is clarity on which perspectives are needed in the room. I find that people can get very good at asking the question, "Do we have everybody that we need in the room?" People quickly develop the capacity to know, together, what perspectives are needed to be able to answer any given question connected to the purpose they serve. That is the first part: what voices do we need? The second part is listening to them. Telling them that they are here, in the room, for a reason. The group needs to know your perspective around this. The group is to hold you to bringing your perspective.

This is a 3-step dance. The first step is whose perspectives. The second step is whether the group can listen authentically and hear what these perspectives are bringing. The third step is in holding each other to the highest standard of what each person is bringing.

In the example of the engineer, marketer, and accountant, the marketer and account do not hold the engineer to marketing standards, rather they hold the engineer to engineering standards.

They hold the accountant to accounting standards, and the marketer to marketing standards. To do that, they must know what that standard is. They require that each other be prepared, to their highest standard, and that they can participate in bringing their perspective, because it is required. This is what we have found, through our global research of the past two decades, in all high-performing groups. These are three steps you can take for engaging the perspectives you need to serve this purpose.

You have experienced many times when this choice of who to include is completely opaque. You have experienced a very low level of the group consciously choosing whose perspectives are needed in the room, to connect and be in service to the deeper purpose. This turns out to be quite normal. I have shared a few informal surveys you can use to test this out. Why do people think they are in the room? What is the group trying to achieve? What is the dominant question the group needs to answer, to achieve that? What perspectives are required to be able to answer that question? Most of these questions are usually answered with, "I don't know. We don't know." Without this clarity, you experience a low level of choosing and honoring those required perspectives. What are the consequences of this low level? If you cannot answer these basic questions of what you are engaging in, you are accessing very low levels of energy, at best, and probably disengaging massive amounts of creative energy. The people in the room who are not engaged, experience that their energy is being wasted. Misdirected. This can lead to most of their attention being directed to self-preservation, a leading cause of burnout. The people who should be in the room, and are not, also experience being excluded. And, by not having the necessary perspectives in the room, the group will make decisions that lack the requisite inputs and lack the requisite understanding and commitment to action. Lots of purposeful energy is wasted and misdirected.

When you experience high levels of choosing the right perspectives to be in the room, you experience a completeness. At these high levels, common practices we have found include: (1) setting the initial conditions of clarifying, for each person, why they are in the room, in the first place, and how to engage with them; (2) robust practices of listening to each perspective, and requiring with them that they bring their best awareness and sharing, using their own standard of excellence; and (3) actively seeking emerging insights, by asking if there were any surprises, spending a few minutes on reflecting and sharing what was seen and what shifted. These are practices for being explicit about what you are starting with, what is happening during the gathering, and where you have shifted to, at the end of the meeting. These are not uncommon practices. Introducing others and their required gifts. Listening and engaging. Asking how that went. You know how to do these, and there are many people you know who are trained in how to do them well. Yet, most gatherings of people do not do these, even though the value of them is clear, as is the cost of not doing them. This is your third choice, to engage the required perspectives in the room.

An Environment of Trust to Share

Your fourth choice within engaging is trust. Are you listening for what you are each bringing? Are you creating an environment where I am supporting you in what you are learning, and where you are supporting me in what I am learning? Your learning and development are important to the group and supporting each other is important. What each person contributes to the group in their creative process is important. This requires creating an environment of trust, so that people can see and share what they already know and what they are learning. They feel that they can actually share.

The people who do this well, whose choices strengthen the engaged energy of the group, support an environment where people share what they are each seeing and learning, from what they know and from what they are learning, and from the possibilities they can see. You are supporting that, so that they share.

You know when you experience low or high levels of trust. You experience less or more of your own self, of others, of the group, of the creative process, of access to creativity itself. You experience these as a vibrancy, a weak to strong vibe. The vibrational excitement of matter and energy, which is straight out of physics. The more excited something gets, the more it vibrates—the more energy it engages. As a being of matter and energy, you also experience this. You are not independent of the physics of it. When more creative energy is being engaged, you can feel it.

In the business case, the excitement (higher energy flowing through) of working through the three perspectives was palpable. We had all the information we needed. We were each bringing our best game, and the others were helping us hold to our standards of excellence. We knew that together we saw far more than any of us did alone. We each brought much greater depth to our own areas of expertise (sales, production, accounting) than even the informed others could access. Much, much more was available to all of us and our decision than if we tried to do this alone. With the dinner party, we each shared more of what we could bring to the setting up of the dinner experience and to what was shared during the dinner.

Most groups don't do this. Someone sets an agenda and then spends the meeting talking at the others. Little to no growth or learning happens in the room, leading to low engagement. For many, the excuse is that they want the meeting to be efficient, meaning quick. This is fine if you don't want people to engage. This, however, begs the question of why have the meeting in the first place. If the meeting is purely to share information, doing it in writing or video might be better, allowing people to think about it, reading or listening as many times as they need, and then post any questions.

Groups who are great at co-hosting an environment of trust, where people engage and share more of who they are and what they are learning are clear about engaging and protecting the experience of the five primary relationships. They engage the individual's already-existing capacities and their learning, with processes that support each other in these sharing explorations. They clarify, continuously, why each perspective is required. They bring creative processes that align with purpose, explore the potential in the unknown, inquire into what is being learned, devour the feedback of what happened, and then collaboratively inquire into what has been learned and might shift, changing what will now be seen and done. They bring out the already-present self, other, group, nature, and spirit. You can use the free, online Agreements Health Check at isclarity. org to assess the level of trust experienced in your group.

You care about creating spaces of trust, where people share what they are there to uniquely contribute. You care about the purpose you are serving. You get excited about learning more because people share what they are also seeing, in their own domains. You experience more of yourself, when you trust, and more of others, when they trust. You care about this. It supports achieving what you want to serve.

You know how to be excited about engaging with curious colleagues who have something specific and relevant to contribute. You know how to listen and support. You know how to learn, on your own and with others. You know how exciting it is to see a possibility, learn from what happens, and adjust. This is your fourth choice, generating spaces of trust, where you and others will share what they already know, what they are learning in the moment, and the vulnerable potentials they can see.

Summary of Choices in Engaging Your Agreements Field

These are three choices you have in engaging the purposeful energy. How you continuously connect to purpose. Whose perspectives are required. An environment of trust for people to share what they know, what they are learning, and possibilities they see.

You care about these three choices to engaging the creative energy already available to you, in service to your deeper shared purpose. You care because you want to serve that purpose. You want your energy to go to that service. You enjoy doing this with others, others who you need. When you do not engage them well, through these choices, consciously or unconsciously, you accept the loss of energy, well over 90% of it. You accept disengaging and self-preservation.

3 CHOICES IN TRANSFORMING ENERGY

You also have three choices in how you transform that engaged energy. Choices in how you structure the connection to that engaged energy, how you structure the transformation of it into something else, and the resilience of your access to the resources those structures require.

Structures of Connection to Engaged Energy

The structures of connection to the energy you have engaged can be understood at three related levels. What you already know—the already finished—which you experience as matter, things, nouns. What you are developing, over time and space—the becoming—which you experience as learning and connecting, the living, the verbs. What you find in potential—the beingness—which you experience as possibility, as something you see in the not-yet-here, in the light-potential.

As a creative being, you continuously work with these three levels. At the noun level, what structures have you put in place to look at, measure, and understand the actual capacities that you already have? The things that you have developed in the past. What you can count on, from before. At the verb level, what structures and processes are in place for your learning? What you are learning now. Processes for adjusting, midstream, based on what you are learning. At the light level, what structures and processes are in place that can support your ability to see new possibilities, and to see how those might inform new pathways or new things to go try to discover what that looks like, getting the feedback and adjusting over time?

Often the structures for connecting to the engaged energy are quite weak. There is only some focus on the available resources, and no attention to what is being learned or to the available possibilities. You often hear, "We don't have time for that." These groups are usually caught off-guard. They are often surprised by what they did not see in resources they already had. You will find lots of duplicated resources, mostly not being used. They are also surprised by lessons they did not learn, where people didn't share something they had learned, because the group did not make space for hearing it and integrating it. This leads to spending lots of time correcting easily avoidable mistakes. As a side note, project management practice shows that many groups spend 80-90% of their time correcting mistakes that they could have avoided with 10% more effort. Highly inefficient. And these groups are often made obsolete by not seeing what was coming from the future. The possibilities were there to see, and they did not. This leads to massive wastes in attention and money that could have been dedicated to something useful that was emerging, which are now thrown away.

Groups with strong structures for connecting to the engaged energy have the resources and decision-making structures that support seeing emerging possibilities, developing new capacities and relationships to manifest those possibilities, and clear measurement and assessment of what happens. They value these different levels, and they have designed social processes that work with them. When aligned with their deeper purpose, in highly engaging ways, these structures connect to all the creative energy that was engaged. This turns out to be far more efficient and effective than not connecting to that engaged energy. These groups access far more energy, because of these structures, which also means that they lose far less of that energy. This puts them at a distinct advantage to groups that lose most of their creative energy.

You know how to work with these high-connection structures. You like seeing possibilities. You like trying out things and learning. You like seeing what you learned. You know how to do most of these, and there are many people you can find in your ecosystem who are good at designing specific pieces of this in highly efficient and effective ways. Your fifth choice is in the information people are bringing about what they already know, what they are learning, and what could be.

Structuring the Transformation of Engaged Energy

You sixth choice is in understanding the functioning of your system. In essence, any system works at three levels. First is the level of direct actions, where A affects B. Pushing the box moved it to another place. Second is the level of feedback loops, where A affects B, which then affects A. The decisions you make today affect your ability to make those same decisions tomorrow. Third is the level of the set of feedback loops. How the feedback loops affect each other and combine to influence your ability to achieve your deeper purpose.

At the level of direct actions, are the specific actions that you are taking done in the most efficient and effective ways? What does excellence there look like? What is the most efficient way for A to influence B? This gets into how you do what you do. What are the lessons learned for the best way to do that, within your specific context?

At the level of feedback loops, are you understanding the dynamics within a specific area? Are you fighting the system, or are you working with the system, seeing the dynamics of how the system works? Are you fighting a snowball? Or are you fighting a balancing energy, the inertia within the system? Are you working with it? Does it strengthen you or weaken you? Working against your system wastes energy. Working with your system leverages your energy. When you understand the feedback dynamics of your system, you can redesign them.

At the level of the set of dynamics, do you know how to coordinate across those dynamics? Is the set of dynamics generating the outcomes and impacts you want? If not, you can work with the interweaving dynamics. If the outcomes remain stable, no matter what you do, a balancing feedback loop is dominating. If the outcomes are accelerating up or down, a reinforcing feedback loop is dominating. By understanding the set of feedback loops you have, you can begin to shift the dominance of the feedback loops, to achieve the shift in impacts you want. You can begin to use the feedback loops to work with each other, using one to support and shift others. These are three levels you can work with in the systemic leverage that you can bring to the transformation of your engaged energy, through your understanding of how the system works, at the direct level, the dynamics level, and coordinating across these dynamics.

Most groups remain very unaware of these three levels of structuring the transformation of engaged energy. With little curiosity and a fixed determination to do things the way they have always been done, groups with weak structures are often quite inefficient in their direct actions. You know this is happening when you expend great amounts of effort and achieve very little in direct outcomes. No matter how much energy you spend yelling at your computer, it does not change its behavior. Chastising your group for weak performance does not show them how to improve it, only how to hide it from you. Groups with weak structures also spend vast amount of energy fighting the system's feedback dynamics. They try to grow against the inertia of a balancing feedback loop. You see this where people open their office windows in the winter because the rooms are too hot. With no control over the thermostat, all they can do is control their local environment, by opening a window and sending the heating bill out the window. Or they try to stabilize a re-enforcing feedback loop. It is rolling down hill: the customers are leaving due to bad service. Giving coupons does not stop this. Or it is growing up too quickly. The teenagers are asking questions and sprouting. Trying to suppress the growth only gets them to submit or leave. The growth still happens, just somewhere else. The consequences of low structural ability to transform the engaged energy means that most of the energy is lost. It is lost to very inefficient uses, which are fighting their very own system. This leads to lots of energy being expended in a system that is fighting itself. A definition of systemic burnout.

In groups that experience strong structures for transforming the engaged energy, they are aware of the three levels. They are constantly understanding and working with their system. To be more efficient in their direct actions, they are continuously looking for and experimenting with actions that work best in that specific context. They are continuously mapping their feedback dynamics and how they work with them. How can they leverage the amount gained in each cycle of the feedback dynamic, making it work even better for them than it did before? They are continuously coordinating how they understand and work with the set of feedback-loop dynamics that define their system, figuring out and testing how to strengthen the dominance of specific feedback mechanisms at any given time. For example, now might be a time for growth, where you want to also be developing the capacities to stabilize support at a future, higher level of performance. You want to grow your customer base, through high levels of service, which you want to be able to sustain going forward, with a much higher service capacity.

You can find people who are trained to support you in the capacity to see, understand, and work with your operating system at these three levels. They study engineering, business, system dynamics. The tools are well developed and relatively easy to work with. You can find examples at isclarity.org, including my own book *Managing from Clarity: Identifying, Aligning and Leveraging Strategic Resources*. This is your sixth choice.

Resilient Structures of Access

Your seventh choice is in transforming around resilience. What resources do you transform into the products and services you provide to serve your purpose? Where do the resources come from, and how are they used? What is the net effect of those flows? How many sources of those resources do you have?

How many uses do you have for the resources going out? Are you generating the resources that you need? Are you dependent on one source? A couple of sources? Do you have multiple sources you can go to to access the resources you need over time and under different circumstances? Or are you generating the resources that you need so that you are resilient to changes in the system for the resources you need?

One simple way of understanding this resource resilience is in funding. Do you have money you need to pay the wages of the people who work for you? At home, to pay your expenses? Is all of that money coming from one source or from many, meaning do you depend on the relationship with one source, or have you access to money through multiple relationships?

Most people experience low resilience most of the time. At the household level this is defined as families that make just enough money every month to cover their basic expenses. Any unseen expense or emergency can throw them off. In many countries, this group is called the middle or lower-middle socioeconomic class, representing over half of the population. In organizations, a low level of resource resilience means that you have enough resources to cover your budget, for now. And, that you will most probably begin to scour for the source of your next budget cycle very soon.

The consequences of low resource resilience are in the effort expended, the relationship dependence, and the attentional requirements of always looking for just enough money. In addition to serving the purpose for which you organized in the first place, you spend great amounts of energy, emotion, and attention on raising monies. If the time frame between inflows and outflows gets erratic, this low-level resilience can easily slip into a frantic mode, which can easily re-orient much attention and effort, possibly collapsing the whole agreements field, focusing it at a low level. A level that makes it difficult to engage in more resource-resilient relationships. Additionally, depending on one source for one's monetary inflow creates a dependency on that relationship, which also tends to influence the rest of the agreements field.

Groups that live with moderate levels of resource resilience tend to have multiple sources of resource inflow, building a network of relationships that support the resource inflows of the group. They might have multiple inflows from products and services, or from donations, membership fees, and services.

Groups that live with high levels of resource resilience tend to generate most of their resource inflows on their own. They have developed systems that regenerate many of the resources they need. The groups we have met at the level of high resilience tend to have developed a deeper purpose that they share across the whole ecosystem they co-lead. They are clear that they are working with larger forces, supporting how creativity and systems work together to generate new possibilities. They are much more focused on the purpose and how they can adjust along the way to achieve it. They create pathways amongst the people and the resources within their ecosystem to access and generate the resources they need now and going forward. This versatility translates into evolving networks of relationships bringing resources to the work. This networking flexibility and diversity of sources for resources provides higher and more sustainable levels of resources making them more resilient.

The skillsets required for high resilience include knowing what your deeper purpose is and how to engage others in contributing to it, inviting, and allowing them to bring their resources and their structures that access resources to the work. You know how to see your purpose and how to engage people in it. Here you open up to the inquiry of what they want to bring to the table, what their skills are, and what resources they have. We want you to come to dinner, what would you like to provide? Salad, dessert, drinks, a game? We are building a school; how would you like to play? Do you teach, are you a builder, do you know regulations, are you a gardener, can you raise funds? There are many resources needed to be more resilient, many forms that can be taken to access those resources, and many ways to generate those resources, on an on-going basis. Therein lies the creativity in resilience, your seventh choice.

Summary of Choices in Transforming in Your Agreements Field

These are the three choices you have in transforming the engaged energy. How you structure your access to the different levels of the engaged energy. How you transform that energy into something else. The resilience you have in accessing the required energy.

You care about these three choices. Having gone to all the effort to engage the available creative energy in the room, the three transforming choices focus you on how to shift that energy's form, how to trans-form it, into a form that better services your purpose. Without that transformation, the engaged energy is lost, and the purpose remains unserved. Very inefficient, especially when transforming it only requires choices you already know how to make.

2 CHOICES IN TRANSFERRING ENERGY

You have two choices in how you transfer the transformed energy. Does the intended recipient want what you are offering, and can they receive it in the form you are offering? Who are your actual recipients, as compared to your stated recipients?

What the Intended Recipients Want and the Form It Takes

The eighth choice you have is in transferring the transformed energy. The focus is on whether the intended recipients of your transformed energy want it. Are the intended recipients engaged with you? Do they want what you are offering? Do they want it in the form that you are offering? Are they able to receive it in the form you are offering?

You can ask them. You can engage with them, and learn what they want, what they need. What is their purpose? How does that purpose determine and define their relationship with you? What drives value for them in what you do? What form do they need it in? Does the language that you use work for them? The offering that you have? Does it serve the outcome the intended recipients are trying to achieve? Do you understand what they want? How they want it? Are they engaged in the process with you? Those are choices you have for the intended recipients of the engaged energy you have transformed.

We find that most groups never ask. They implicitly think that, as experts in what they do, they know more than the intended recipients about what the intended recipients actually want. This is one of the old adages of business: figure out what they want before they do, then convince them that is what they want. While there is often great innovation in looking for the next thing that might provide even greater value to the intended recipient, this mindset seems to often come with an attitude of knowing better than the recipient. This leads to very, very low levels of direct, strategic engagement with the recipient. They will engage with the recipient to give them the product or service, while not engaging the recipients by asking them what they want. Though marketing intelligence is a large field, few people take the time to inquire with the intended recipient, at all. The consequences of low levels of engagement with the intended recipient is low take-up. And when they do take it up, the value they perceive from it is low, because it does not fit in with the way they see the world. Fine, I will accept your donated clothes. I will take classes in your program. I will pay for what you offered, but the value to me is far less than it could be, if you would have asked what I really wanted, and offered it in a form that was much more useful to me.

And, we have found groups that are very good at this, experiencing high levels of engagement with the intended recipients. These groups involve the intended recipients of their products or services from the very beginning, in collaboratively defining the why, in understanding what perspectives are needed and who best provides them. They dedicate a lot of time to understanding the intended recipient's context, from the recipient's perspective, with the recipient. What does a thriving child mean for your family, in your community? What does success look like? What are the challenges faced, in your community, in achieving that success? In what ways do you talk about it? When thinking about the gathering of our friends, what are you most looking for? What do you most enjoy? What would make it easiest for you to say Yes! to engaging? What would make it a Big Yes! for you?

If you care about your Yes!, and you care about the intended recipients of your efforts, you might enjoy working with them to understand what they actually want and the form that best serves what they value. You know about the topic. You know how to ask questions and listen. You know who to engage. This is your eighth choice.

Your E^3, Your Everyone Everywhere Everyday

Your ninth choice is in the transferring dimension of your E^3. Your Everyone Everywhere Everyday. $E_1{}^*E_2{}^*E_3=E^3$. Who do you think you are serving? Who are you actually serving? Could you state that you are serving who you are actually serving? What geographies or demographies are you saying that you serve, as compared to those you are actually serving? How much of the time do you say you are serving them, as compared to what you are actually doing? What are the choices that you are making? What do you say that you are actually in service to? Are you doing what it takes to shift, if you are not actually doing it?

Most groups define a target group for their work. All our friends, for the dinner party. All kids who live in the state, for the public K-12 education system. You can decipher this statement of the intended target group to mean that it is for everyone in that specific ecosystem, whether the dinner party or the public-school system, everywhere within the different socio-demographic hills and valleys of the ecosystem, every day. For everyone all the time, within that specified ecosystem. This is the desired E^3. Everyone (E_1) everywhere (E_2) everyday (E_3) equals 100%. Everyone.

Then there is the reality of who the system actually serves. It serves some of your friends, some of the time. The vegetarians and friends with little kids never seem to make it to the dinner party. The intention was there, but the reality showed up different. The public K-12 education system is to support the thriving for all kids living in this state, but only half of them are thriving in the system. This is the actual E^3. Some of the people (E_1) in some of the socio-demographics (E_2) some of the time (E_3). E^3 is 50%, which is far less than 100%. The stated purpose of the system is not what the system actually does. It serves some of the people well some of the time. It does not serve some of the people at all, and none of the people all the time.

Most groups live with a low E^3. The people they say they intend to serve are not served to the desired level. This often causes an erosion of goals. Oh well, we wanted to serve all the kids, but it did not work, so we will be happy if we can serve half of them. This is the life of many groups. People working with these groups often start with very high aspirations, intrigued by the stated purpose. As they discover their actual E^3 over time, their capacity to engage and give their lives to the work wanes. They are not serving the purpose they thought they were, to the degree they thought they were.

This leads to a major challenge for the groups. They have supposedly designed their organization and invited people to engage in serving a community that they are not serving. This means one of two things. It could be that their organization is spending resources towards a much higher level than they are achieving, which means they are getting far less impact for the same investment. They are inefficient at what they do. Or it could be that the way they designed their system cannot achieve its intended purpose. They are ineffective in what they do. Whether for reasons of efficiency or effectiveness, both are a call for redesigning the agreements that guide their ecosystem. If the system is not doing what it was intended to do—the E^3 is less than 100%—then you can redesign your system for E^3 equals 100%.

We have also found many groups with very high E^3. They are constantly engaging the many different types of recipients they have, in the many socio-demographic niches of their ecosystem (E_2). They are constantly experimenting with ways to adapt their offering for different needs. They are also clear on who they serve. They stay away from broad statements of serving everyone, focusing on who they want to and are able to serve.

The question here focuses on the choice to align who your system is actually serving and who it needs to serve. You can either narrow your intended recipients to what your system actually does or change your system to meet all your intended recipients. That is your ninth choice.

Summary of Choices in Transferring in Your Agreements Field

These are the choices you have in an agreements field. This gives you these nine choices in how you engage, how you transform, and how you transfer that energy. You have nine choices that you can make.

Choice Number	Agreements Field Dimension	Choice	Cost of No! (low level)	Benefit of Yes! (high level)
1	Transferring purpose	What deeper purpose	Weak energy source	Strong energy source
2	Engaging connection to purpose	How connect to that purpose	Not plugged in	Constant connection to energy source
3	Engaging perspectives	Whose perspectives are need for this purpose	Most dimensions of energy are missing	Higher order of energy available
4	Engaging trust	An environment of trust to share	Little sharing	Deep sharing and trust
5	Transforming connection to engaged energy	Structures of connection to engaged energy	Access to existing capacities only	Access to deep potential, development, and evolving capacities
6	Transforming structure	Structuring the transformation of engaged energy	Low leverage through disparate units	High leverage through coordinated dynamics and integrated units
7	Transforming resilience	Resilient structures of access	Vulnerability to weak access to resources	Resilience through regenerative resources
8	Transferring connection to recipients	What the intended recipients want and the form it takes	Weak, low-value acceptance of offer	Deep co-evolution of offer with recipients
9	Transferring E^3	Your everyone, everywhere, everyday	Few infrequently served	All served continuously

Table 1: Choices in Transferring Energy

Net Yes! leads to net positive. No! leads to net negative. Now you know. You know it is your choice. You know the nine dimensions of your agreements field, your Yes! You know the massive costs of No! And the benefits of Yes! Your Yes! What processes can support you in shifting your existing agreements to align with your Yes!?

SHIFTING AGREEMENTS FIELDS

The nine choices you have in your agreements field. So far we have seen how to work with the purposeful energy in your agreements field. What is this purposeful energy? How do you align with it? What does it mean for you? Why do you care? Do you care about closing the gap between where you are and where it needs to be? We have also looked at the agreements field dimensions of engaging, transforming, and transferring the energy and the nine choices you have in each of the dimensions of your agreements field.

TOOL–BEHAVIOR OVER TIME GRAPH

Now we want to look at how you shift your agreements field. What are the choices you have in shifting it? Let's look at a tool and a process that guide you in shifting your agreements field.

Let's look at the tool first. It is a Behavior-over-Time (BoT) graph. The purpose of this graph is to look at the goal that you state you are here to serve. How you use your purposeful energy to generate something in service to someone. How well are you doing? How have you done in the past? How will you probably do in the future? What does it need to be if you are actually in service? If your $E^3=100\%$? What is the difference?

What will it take to close that gap? What is the scale of what you have achieved? What is the scale of what needs to happen to achieve your purpose? Over what time horizon, to be in service to this purposeful energy?

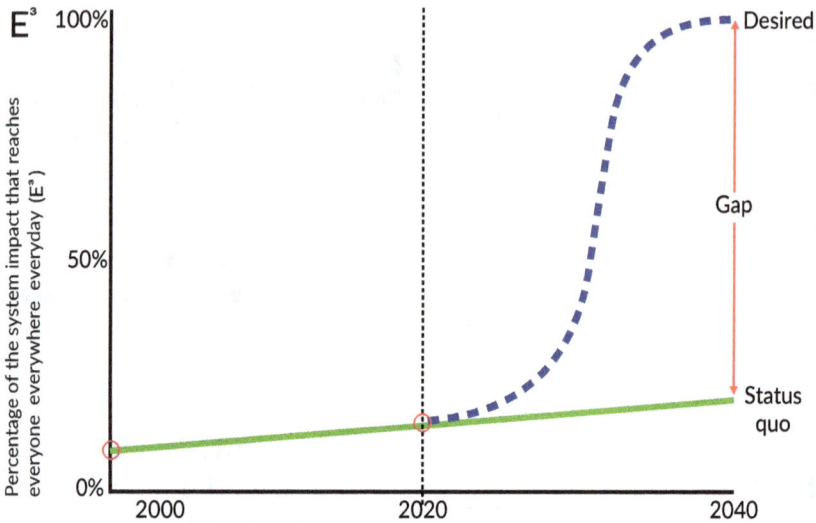

Figure 7: Behavior Over Time (BoT) Graph for E^3

The Measure of Purpose (the Y-axis)

The first step in drawing the BoT graph describes your purposeful energy. What purpose are you serving in the system? This is the organizing principle for why the system exists.

What is a measure for how well the system is doing that? Is it the number of kids scoring proficient or better on the state exam? Is it some measure of thriving in the state? The number of children thriving? The level of thriving of each individual within the state's K-12 public education system? Is it the level of fellowship experienced in our dinner party? Is it the quality of my listening with my children? Whatever that energy that pulls the system together is. What is it that you are measuring?

The BoT in Figure 7 describes a system's impact on its intended community, expressed in term of its E^3, how well it positively impacts everyone in the intended ecosystem, everywhere within the ecosystem, all the time.

The second step in drawing the BoT graph describes the scale of that purposeful energy. What does a very high level look like? What does a very low level look like? These questions calibrate the ends of the measurement. This allows you to know whether you are scoring very high on this dimension or very low. What is the percentage of thriving kids? What percentage of the kids score proficient or better on our state exam in Massachusetts? What is the level of thriving of all children in the state? What is the level of fellowship at our dinner party?

This can either be a qualitative or quantitative measure. It is a proxy, an approximate measure of something, with which you can start this exploration. For example, very high might look like 100% of the kids are thriving, and very low looks like 0% of the kids are thriving. You can have a description for high thriving and a description for very low thriving. What would low fellowship and very high fellowship look like at your dinner party?

I also find it useful in describing the low and high ends of the continuum to paint a scenario of what that looks like. This gives you a feeling for that reality. What does thriving look like in Massachusetts if all children are thriving? How would we know we were in that world? You can paint a brief picture of that scenario, that worldview, that world, that universe. You can do the same for the low end of the continuum. What would a world look like and feel like if none of the children in Massachusetts were thriving? You can also do this for the midpoint. What does 50% look like? What does halfway between the very low and the very high ends of the continuum look like? Where half of the kids are thriving or many of the kids are thriving some of the time. With the very high, the very low, and the midpoint, you have a scale for determining where you are in achieving your purpose.

This describes the vertical Y-axis of Figure 7. The relevant range for E^3 is its full continuum, from the very low level where nobody is met anywhere in the system ever, E^3 equals 0%, to the very high level where everybody is met everywhere in the system every day, E^3 equals 100%.

The third step in the BoT Graph describes where you are today. On the scale, from very high to very low on the purpose, you look at today. Where are you today on this scale? You can start by asking yourself this question. You can get different people that know something about the system to give their opinions. If this is what high looks like, with this description of the universe of your purpose, this is what low looks like, and this is what the midpoint looks like, where would you say that we are today? What evidence would you provide to say that this is where you think we are today? On that scale, with that measure? I find that, generally, if I can get people who know something about the system agreeing to this proxy, you get pretty close in agreeing on where you are today on that continuum. You can also see how much variance there is in your opinions about where you are today. Are you all pretty close, in agreement? Are there big differences? Exploring the differences potentially highlights differences in perspectives, providing a richer picture. This is the choice you have in engaging perspectives.

In Figure 7, the level today is low, around 15%. This is depicted where the dotted, vertical line above today, on the horizontal X-axis, meets the green solid line.

The fourth step is, where do you need to be? Going back to your purposeful-energy question, what is it that the system is actually designed for? Your E^3=100%. The desired level. Where do you know that you need to be?

I asked this question for the state of Massachusetts K-12 public-education system. Do you want to improve beyond 52% to 70% or 80%? The group responded "No! This is the public education system, for all kids in the state of Massachusetts. Kindergarten through 12th grade, so it needs to serve all of them. 100%." Good, so then what? Now you can start to say where you need to be versus where you are right now.

In Figure 7, the reason the group is getting together to look at this question of the E^3 is that this very low level is not the intention. The intention is for E^3 to be 100%. That is the very reason for the system and all of its effort.

Over What Time Horizon (X-Axis)

The fifth step is to decide over what time horizon you believe that you can actually make this change. This question is not asking you what is reasonable to do. It never can be reasonable, because you have never before achieved what you are here to achieve now. If it were already reasonable to do, it would have been done already.

That is why you are here now. It is also not a "get it done in the next year" panacea, if there is no way to change the whole system within one year. With this said, they also thought it was impossible to get to the moon within a decade when John F. Kennedy gave his famous moonshot speech. Yet, within the decade, they did. So, what are the conditions that you have? Even if it takes a lot of work, under what time horizon could you get it? Is it in the next year? The next five years? The next ten years or twenty years? How big is the system you are working with? How complex is it? Even with very concentrated collaborative efforts, what do you think is possible?

This gives you two approaches. One approach is what you think is possible, if you are able to get everybody aligned. A second approach is what you have to do, because you do not have a choice. You have to be able to do this. That helps you organize your efforts. This is a very serious effort. You have to be able to achieve this, within this time horizon. You see this in examples of when a country goes to war, or when people are getting ready to have a child. Something beautiful is happening, or something ugly is happening. You do not have ten years to plan for this child. This child will be here with you in nine months. So, now, what are you going to do? Or when the competition makes a move. You cannot say, well we have five years to plan this out. It is now. How are you going to react and by when? You need a response.

In the E^3 example, in Figure 7, if this can be shifted, for this particular system, within a generation, then the BoT maps out twenty years to the left and right of today. Looking forward, if the system continues to operate in the same way that it does today, E^3 is expected to continue to increase, very slowly over the next twenty years to maybe 20%. The question then is how to get from the 15% E^3 of today to the E^3 of 100% within twenty years. The BoT captures the discussion that E^3 needed to shift quickly, to much higher levels within the next few years, then leveling out and sustaining at the higher, more appropriate level of 100%.

The sixth step in the BoT graph description is to look backwards over that same time horizon. If you looked forward five to ten years, now look back five to ten years. Where were you, on that same continuum of high to low? Where were you then? Were you at the same level, higher, lower? You can ask people to give you their opinions. You can see what the differences are in their opinions about where you were back then. Ask them to explain where they think you were.

You go back the same amount of time as you go forward to help you see relevant patterns. If you go back in Step 6 much further than you went forward in Step 5, you will highlight long-term patterns that might not be relevant in the shorter future horizon and miss shorter dynamic patterns that will be relevant. The same happens if you go back less time than you went forward. You now have a time horizon, with today in the middle, that will highlight relevant patterns of systemic dynamics.

The BoT in Figure 7 captures that the E^3 twenty years ago was a bit lower, at approximately 10% and has only slightly increased over the past twenty years.

The seventh step is to describe how you moved between where you were back then and where you are now. You are looking for the trend. Was it at the same level as today? Higher? Lower? Was the path from the past to today one of a gradual decline? A gradual increase? Was there a lot of effort put in that shifted up, for a short period? Did it oscillate, with little efforts that tried and that failed? What was the trend between then and now? That gives you a sense of how the system responds to initiatives, to how well the system of your agreements field performed in the past.

Figure 7 captures that the E^3 twenty years ago was a bit lower, at approximately 10% and has only slightly increased over the past twenty years.

This brings you to a big insight from systems theory. The system that you have, from the past to today, generated the outcome on this measure that you have, for the purpose of your system. The system you have today is perfectly designed to generate this behavior. It does it well. That is its E^3=100%. Independent of what you say the system is designed to do, it is designed for E^3=100%. For those people, in those demographies, for that amount of the time. That is what it is doing. You have also stated that it needs to be at a different level, in the future. That your system needs to do something different than what it was designed to do. You need another design. New agreements.

Looking at chronic disease across United States, tens of millions of years of life are lost by the poor each year due to chronic disease. These are years they would not lose if they were not poor. That number needs to be dramatically reduced, and it is reducible. In Vermont, none of the energy was being generated within the state, and it needed to be for Vermonters to have sovereignty over their energy decisions. For dengue, it was demonstrably clear that every time dengue came into Mexico there was an epidemic, an outbreak. To get a different behavior than the one that the system is perfectly designed to generate, you need a different system. You know that the system is perfectly designed to do what it does, because that is what you have experienced for the life of that system, which you just traced.

Now for the eighth step. If you do not change anything, what is the most probable future? You have to be careful in what you mean by "not changing anything." This means that you continue to do what you are doing today. It does not mean that you do nothing. You continue to act in the system the way you are now. You are still doing all the initiatives that exist to-day, in the same way. The other way you now have of saying this is that you continue the same activity with the same agreements. If you do not change how you are interacting, if the system continues to be perfectly designed the way it is today, then where will you probably end up? Map that out. Will that most-probable future be gradual, increase, stay the same, or decrease? What will you need to do to get there and be able to sustain the new level, so that it does not collapse back to its current level?

In Figure 7, the most probable result of not changing anything would be only a slight increase, over the next two decades, of the number of people included in the E^3, reaching some more people, in some more of the socio-demographic areas, some of the time.

Looking forward, there is a gap. This is the ninth step. A gap between where you will go if you stay with the status quo, the way you are working now, and where you need to go. Does this gap motivate you? How important is it to you to close this gap? This is the motivating force for change. This is the gap that you have to organize around, changing your agreements.

The agreements you have generated created the past that you have experienced. These agreements you have will also generate the status quo future. You need different agreements to generate a different outcome. You know this because your current agreements generated what you experienced. And, you want a different experience, a different outcome. You know that you do not know what those new agreements are, because you have not achieved them. If you knew what those agreements were, you would probably be living into them. And you are not. This is what you have just drawn in the BoT graph. That is the tool's power.

In the E^3 story (Figure 7), what is the driving force for change to close the gap between the status quo, low level of E^3 and the desired level of 100%?

With nine steps (Table 2), you can describe your Yes! and the motivating force for change.

Step	BoT Graph Element	What Elements Shows
1	Y-axis label	Your purpose
2	Scale of Y-axis. High scenario, low scenario, midlevel scenario	What great, okay, and not realities of different choices look like
3	Today. Where you are now on the Y-axis	Your current reality
4	Future desired level	Where you need to be
5	Time horizon to required change	Time horizon for change
6	Where you were X time units in the past	Where you were when you started
7	How you moved from the past to today	What your past efforts achieved
8	Status quo future	What happens if you continue the way you are now
9	The gap, between your status quo and desired futures	Your motivating force for change

Table 2: Process and Choices in 9-Step Development of the BoT Graph

PROCESS—AGILE VIBRANCY MOVE

What do those new agreements look like? You can also think about the choices you have to shift to achieve these new agreements. To think about shifting agreements, you can use the agile vibrancy move process.It is framed around the agile software idea of prototyping. Basically, test and see.

You start the process by remembering that the experience of the next level of agreements is not something that you are living today, because you are not getting that outcome and not having that experience now. The underlying assumptions you have about the world, the agreements that you have about your interactions determine, to a great part, the experience you have and the outcomes you achieve. The assumptions underlying each level of agreements are very different at each level. Combining the agreements-field framework with the hundreds and hundreds of groups studied globally over the past twenty years points at what those underlying assumptions look like. These assumptions differ in the capacities they bring in to see what you have from the past, the already-finished nouns, what you perceive and what you are learning over time, the becoming verbs, and the potential light. The different levels require different economic resources, different political, decision-making processes, different cultural values and decision-making and decision-enforcement criteria, and different social forms of interacting, different rules of the game.

What you need to step into, to align your Yes! towards the desired, future state is different than what you are already doing, otherwise you would already be experiencing that new level. Instead of trying to understand what assumptions and agreements you need to shift, based on what you are doing now, you can ask a different question. You know what the gap is. You know that it is important to you to close this gap. That is the first step.

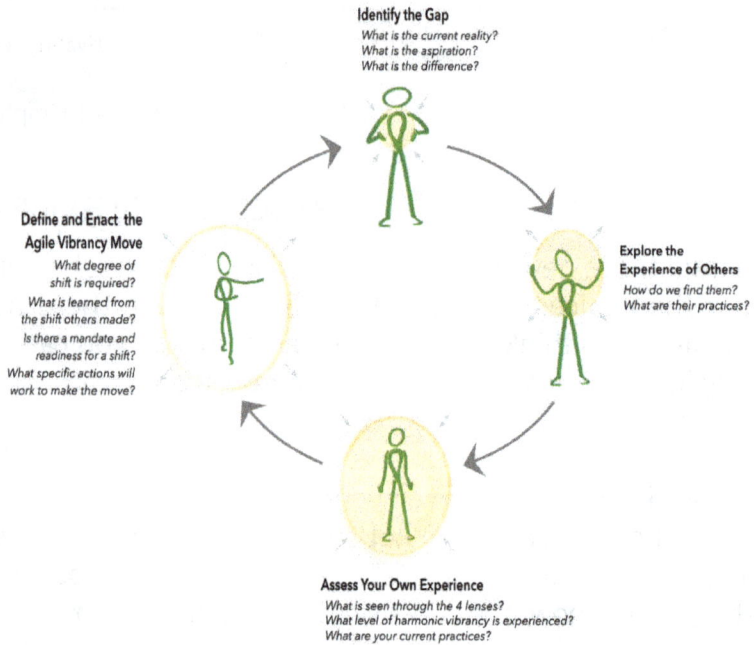

Identify the Gap
What is the current reality?
What is the aspiration?
What is the difference?

Explore the Experience of Others
How do we find them?
What are their practices?

Assess Your Own Experience
What is seen through the 4 lenses?
What level of harmonic vibrancy is experienced?
What are your current practices?

Define and Enact the Agile Vibrancy Move
What degree of shift is required?
What is learned from the shift others made?
Is there a mandate and readiness for a shift?
What specific actions will work to make the move?

Figure 8: Agile Vibrancy Move Process

The second step explores what life looks like at the next level. You know that you are not doing that, because you are not living that next level now. What does life look like at that next level? What kinds of agreements do they have in agreements fields that are able to generate the kind of experience that you desire? What does that experience look like? You have already described that scenario for yourself, in Step 2 of the Behavior over Time graph process. What the world at that next level looks like. A world of thriving children, of deep fellowship at dinners, of listening deeply to my child. Whatever that next experience is, do you have any experiences of groups that are experiencing something like that? Do you know places where all the students are thriving? It might be a very small system. It might be a difference of what they do. Now you can look for similar experiences to that desired scenario. Whether in the K-12 education system, or at a different kind of school. Do you know a group where everybody is thriving? What does that look like? Do you have friendship groups where they have deep fellowship? You know what that experience looks like and feels like. You described the scenario in Step 2 of the Behavior over Time graph process. Where else have people experienced that feeling? Ask.

Once you begin to think of groups or places where you have experienced something like the desired scenario you described, you can now go and see. See what life looks like there. This is important for two reasons. First, they are doing something different than what is happening right now in your system. That is why they are getting different outcomes and having different experiences. That is how you know that.

The second reason is critical, at this stage of the process. This is the choice of what you are able to shift in your system, from within your system. What you can do within your system, and what you know. Experience clearly shows what does not work. When people tell you what they think you should do. It never works. Never. Because you cannot actually do what they think you should do. Why? Because when they talk at you, they are demonstrating that they do not know what your context is, and they do not know if you are ready to do it. They cannot know if you are ready to do it, or if you already know how to do it, or if you are already doing it. As a wise Bolivian farmer told me once, "I do not know what you know. I do not know what you do not know. Only you can know that." Knowing this, the philosopher-farmer would invite people to come see what he was doing, for themselves. Likewise, you can go see the other system. You can see what you notice that they are doing that is different. If you can notice what they are doing that is different than what you are doing, this gives you a choice, for you.

This is a very simple observation. You cannot notice something in somebody else that you do not have, somehow, the inner skillset for. That does not mean you know how to do it now, or that you are good at doing it. It does mean that, since you noticed it, you have some degree of awareness of it. Some of the elements of it clicked in your mental model of the world, in your sensemaking. You noticed it, so you have some capacity to be able to step into it, to recognize it. Now you can ask questions. This is what you observed of what they are doing now.

In the E^3 narrative, described above and captured in Figure 7, your first step of the agile vibrancy move process declares your deeper shared purpose and defines the gap between the future that will result from your current agreements and the necessary state. The level of E^3 needs to shift from its current, low state to 100%. Step 2 asks if there is a place or a group that you know where they are achieving an E^3 of 100%, they are serving the entire community they intend to serve. If you do not know of such a group, ask. Someone in your community, or someone they know, will very probably know of such a group. You can then visit with that group to see what it is in their agreements that allows them to achieve $E^3 = 100\%$. What do you notice? What is different about what they do than what you do?

In the third step, you come back and look at what you do, in your own agreements. How are your agreements different from what you observed they were doing? This highlights what you noticed. It puts it in reference to your existing agreements.

In the fourth step, you explore what you can do to start trying some of what they were doing. You can pay attention to what that does within your system. This is the agile process, prototyping. Go try that.

For example, what you noticed about what they do in the school where the kids seem to all be doing really well. They have a different approach to how they see children. They do not have attendance problems. They do not have attention problems within the classroom. What are they doing? I observed this when I visited my daughter's kindergarten class twenty-odd years ago. I had been teaching as a university professor for six years at the time. I often had discipline problems with the adults in my MBA classes. Not paying attention, not being on time, being disrespectful of each other, of the process. Watching a kindergarten class, with twenty little kids, my daughter included, and the teacher did not have any of these discipline problems. I had had my daughter's friends over, so I knew what having five or six five-year-old kids running around was like. That was not happening in this classroom with all these kids. What was I able to see? I noticed the teacher was doing something different than I did. The way she was paying attention to them was different. She was watching and giving them a lot of freedom to do what they wanted. She watched them do it, the way they wanted to do it, until something started to take them off purpose. Until there started to be certain kinds of friction. She allowed some and not others. She would "all of a sudden" start to guide them into purposeful activity. She only helped them engage in purposeful activity at touch points. This enabled them to engage more fully, in what they were doing, in ways that were beyond their own capacity to see. She was not mandating. She was not yelling. She was not blowing the whistle at them. She was not correcting them. She was guiding them into the behaviors that they actually wanted. They just did not know how to get there.

That experience shifted completely how I saw my classroom. My perception of what was I doing. I saw that my students were engaged, that they wanted to be there. They wanted to listen to each other. Not because I told them to, but because they chose to. How could I see when that was veering off? What were the tools I had to be able to reengage them toward what they were actually there to do when they were with me in the classroom? This was a completely different experience. One that I had wanted and not known how to produce. Nothing from my previous years of experience guided me. Seeing it in her allowed me to see it in me. Now I was ready to go and experience, in my classroom with my students, and see what happened.

The fifth step in the agile vibrancy move process is to get the feedback in seeing the gap now. To observe the outcomes. The nouns. The feedback the system is giving you, for what you tried. What is that showing you, in the shift in your behaviors, the shift in your assumptions, your agreements, your interactions, your experience, your behaviors? Your outcomes and outputs. Now what can you see? What will you try next? Go try something else, another future possibility, and see how that works. What does that now bring up in your system? It is a continuous process. An evolutionary process of shifting how you are, what do you can see, what you can understand, now, based on those experiences. What do you want to try? Is that working to help you shift your system from where it is to where it needs to be, so that it is aligned with your Big Yes!?

You have all these choices around your purpose and aligning with it, with the different dimensions of the agreements field, with engaging, transforming, and transferring that energy, with seeing what your big purpose is, and whether you are aligned towards it. You can see and shift those agreements. That is the agile vibrancy move.

These are choices that you have in your agreements field. Those that can align you with your Yes! You are aligning your underlying assumptions, agreements, interactions, experience, and outcomes with a Yes! You are moving towards the net positive. That is what you are seeking.

ALIGNING YOUR OPERATING SYSTEM WITH YOUR YES!

WHERE ARE WE?

What have we covered so far? You start with your initial conditions. You start with a Yes! or a No! You choose or accept a Yes!, or you choose or accept a No!, to human creativity, to love for the future to which you give your will. You saw the implications of that. Of ending up in net negative, or in net positive. No! or Yes! You saw that many people were doing this, saying Yes!, figuring out how to look at the agreements they have. What they can do. How to know when you are in an agreement that is a Yes! or a No! You prefer Yes agreements to No agreements. What are agreements? You looked at the agreements field. You looked at different dimensions of the SCAN of your agreements field. You saw the choices in how to engage your agreements field. The choices you had in your agreements field, in the purpose that you are serving. You then started to look at how you could shift your agreements field from where it is to where you need it to be. Do you know what is yours to do? The Behavior over Time graph is a tool to help you see the gap between the outcomes and impacts of your current agreements and the outcomes and impacts you need to achieve, in alignment with your Yes! You looked at the agile vibrancy move process to see what it is, what it needs to be, and what agreements look like at that next level. These are all the components, if you like, of your Yes! operating system.

What is your Yes! operating system? Let's start with understanding what your operating system does and why you have one, then we can look at specific processes and tools you can use to work with it.

WHAT YOUR OPERATING SYSTEM DOES

Why does your Yes! operating system exist, in the first place? It helps you grow, continuously, over time, individually and as a group. Growth is good. You want to see growth. In the first years of life, as a physical being, starting as a very small being and growing to your full size. You also want to grow in your health as a biological being, getting stronger and fitter as you age. You want to grow as a caring being and as a thinking being, in your ability to embrace more and more people and more and more complexity. You want to grow in the impact that you can have. Growth is good. Growth in time and growth in space. Growing stronger and healthier, into your full potential, as a thinking, feeling, willing, physical being.

You also grow in space. You grow over the number of people and agreements fields. The circles of embrace and the number of generations that you can include, of people younger and older than you. How do you grow the impact of your work, on more people in your immediate family, on friendships, on your colleagues at work or church, in your sports teams? How many different groups can you include?

Why do you want to think of having a Yes! operating system? To achieve this growth in time and space, to grow stronger, healthier, with greater expression of your unique, beautiful creativity to engage more of yourself, as you continue to develop over a lifetime, growing the number of people that you influence and embrace, the number of generations you can bring into your work together, all of this is an expansion of your influence.

To achieve this continuous growth and impact, you are following a strategy. Do you know what it is? Have you consciously chosen it? Or have you unconsciously accepted it? It is written in your operating system. What are the outputs and the impacts of what you do? The difficulty with having a strategy is how to know what it is and how to test it. Many things you do you think must be good things to do. Or maybe you just do them without thinking about them. Things you think that might be good things to do, because you saw somebody else do them, or because the idea just came to you. How do you know, within the context of your life, of your communities, whether this intervention, this new thing that you are trying, this thing that you are growing towards, is leading towards what you think it is?

You can also think that about this as testing your hypotheses, testing your strategy. Recent research brings together findings from modern medicine to the wisdom traditions, showing that you can indeed adjust your operating system, and that shift can lead to very significant changes in your experience and outcomes, physically, relationally, emotionally, mentally.

Normally you cannot do this, because you do not understand how these different pieces fit together. Of the things that you do, and how those affect the outputs of your whole system. How those impact others within your ecosystem. For example, what if you are trying to eat better. If you do not know how to understand what is changing, you might think that you feel better. Is it because you are changing your blood, or changing your temperature, or changing your muscle tone, or changing your bowels? Is it changing your brain functioning? Your breathing? Those are very different systems, so unless you have a way of understanding how to think about the impacts of what you are doing in each of them, as a whole set, it is difficult to parse this out. The facts of these causes are very difficult, if not impossible, to distinguish what the different interventions are doing, often at the same time. These are hypotheses that make up your strategy for how you align your system to get the outcomes you want, in your service to your purpose, your Yes! And you can test your strategy. How can you test your strategy? By developing a definition of your operating system.

An operating system is the system with which you operate. With which you make things work. To operate literally means to do something. Something in the system, the set of elements that you have, and the ways that they relate to the purpose. What is the purpose, what you are trying to achieve, what is the organizing principle for how you put things together?

Your Yes! operating system is your agreements field. Your Big YES! operating system. The system with which you do things, and cause things to happen in the world. How can you understand what this operating system is? This infrastructure that you use. The physical, biological, and social, in the intellectual and spiritual realms of your life. What we have been calling your agreements field.

Without this operating system description of what you are, how the different parts relate to each other, in space and time, you cannot test your strategies. You can see if eating this particular food changes anything. If you do not know what it is supposed to change, or how to measure the change, you do not know if it is going to change your biology. How do you know if it is changing your emotions or your thoughts? It is possible to know, if you think about how to do it. This is what a lot of people have learned.

Agreements field mapping is starting to clarify one way to do this. You can test your strategy. You can test the strategy of how what you are going to do is leading to something. You can see if it works. You can learn and adjust. Learning and adjusting is also called evolving. Learning and adjusting, so that you are different after you tried something. You learned and you evolved. The learning and evolving is how you adjust your reality to align it with your Yes!

USING YOUR OPERATING SYSTEM TO TEST YOUR BIG YES! STRATEGY

To test your strategy, with your operating system, you have five different pieces of your operating system (see Figure 9). Five levels where you can intervene to make choices, to align your reality, with your Yes! First there is the direct intervention of the thing that you do. Whether it is eating a piece of fruit, taking a walk, saying hello to a friend, or giving yourself something to write. That is a *direct intervention*, the input.

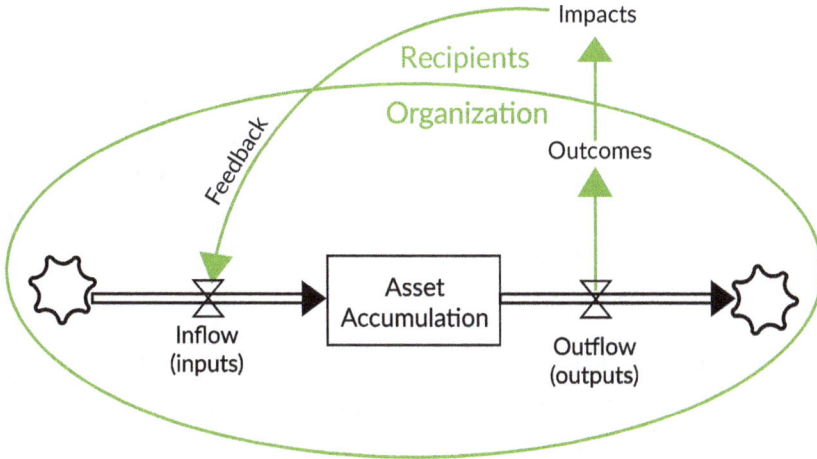

Figure 9: Five Levels of Intervention

Second there are intermediate or process elements. These are what happens when you do something. So, eating leads to satisfying hunger, and to nurturing, putting nutrients into your body. This influences the chemistry of your body. Talking to your friend increases fellowship and trust. Spending time walking is influencing the flow of your metabolism, things moving through your body. Giving yourself time to write, produces material for a book or an article. These process elements are *outputs*. What are the outputs of what you are doing? You have certain levels of sugars or energy in your body. You have spent hours in fellowship with friends. You have written books. These activities that you are doing, your direct interventions, are affecting these processes or activities, which over time lead to outputs, measures of the result of that activity.

Third, what is the *outcome* of those outputs? Measured within the frame of the inputs and outputs of the processes. You feel more energetic from the sugar. You experience fellowship with your friends. You have shared your experience with your books.

The fourth level moves beyond the local content of your immediate agreements field to the agreements fields of others, the space of their agreements field, and agreements with you or on their own. This is the *impact* on others of your activities. What is the quality of the experience, the value experienced somewhere else in the ecosystem, of having done that? What was the impact of having eaten? Having the energy enabled something to happen. What was the impact of the walking? Of the trust in your friendships? The impact of developing those books? You can start to look at what others value, what other parts of the ecosystem value of what you are doing. The extension into the space of others of your Yes! The impact of your efforts.

And, finally, the fifth. There is *feedback*. There is looking at the direct interventions (or inputs), outputs, outcomes, and impacts. There is having ways to assess them. See how those assessments help you understand what is happening in the system, the system's reaction to your intervention.These are the "sacred nouns" the universe provides. It is feedback. What happens when you take an idea from the realm of infinite potential, and you enact it, you act it into the world. This was a thought you had. This was an action you took, an activity over time. The universe actually gives you feedback, on each of these dimensions. This brings out two questions. Are you looking for this feedback, and are you doing something with that feedback, that sacred noun? The fifth element is feedback.

Did eating this make you feel better or weaker? Did engaging with your friends this way and this amount of time lead to deeper relationship, deeper trust, deeper ability to depend on each other? Did having these ideas, in writing these materials lead to this community impact and people taking up the work? What was the feedback that you received? That is the fifth element of your operating system. With this feedback, you have a choice. You can shift your agreements field, aligning your reality with your Yes! Without this feedback, you do not see to shift your agreements field. This feedback is part of your superpower, your Yes!

MAPPING YOUR OPERATING SYSTEM

These are the basic elements you want to map in your Yes! operating system. The first is the purpose, as seen in the previous chapter, your deeper shared purpose. What is it that you are really here to do? What is it you know that the bringing together of all these efforts is yours to do? Whether it is you individually or as a group. What is it you know that you are here to do? The Yes! that you are giving your energy towards. That is your purpose. What is a proxy for that? How do you know if this is the organizing principle of the system, of your agreements field, of this operating system?

With this operating system of inputs, outputs, outcomes, impacts, and feedback, you can test your strategy of what to do to serve your Yes!, of how to align your reality with your purpose, your Yes! Without your operating system, you cannot test your strategy.

Now you can start to map the direct actions that you take, and how these actions are measured in outputs, effort done, and then how those outputs influence the outcomes that are expected from these activities. And the impacts on other parts of the ecosystem, the value they experience from these outputs. Then the feedback mechanisms that pull all of this together.

The GRASP framework helps pull these elements together into a scorecard. GRASP stands for Goals, Resources, Actions, Structure, and People. What is the goal? The global goal, the purpose. This is the deeper shared purpose, the Yes! What are the value-driving resources? These are the outcomes and impacts. What are the enabling resources, the basic ingredients you start with? These are the inputs. What are the actions that you can take? There are the activities, measured in outputs. In summary, what are the goals, resources, and actions? What structure unites these elements, that pulls together the links causally? What are the incentives that people have?

You Try. For example, now with your own big Yes! scorecard. Start with the question for yourself. What is it that you are really here to do? What does success look like, for you? What does better look like for you? What is your Yes!? This may take many iterations. That is called learning. Development. One of the biggest gifts that you can give yourself is to pay attention to where you are now. Are you using a Big Yes! that is yours, now? Are you operating with a Big Yes! that was yours a long time ago? Are you not even thinking about it? Going by the seat of your pants? That is all fine. You have the opportunity, in any given moment, to ask yourself of yourself, what is your Big Yes!? What is it now, given where you are, what you have learned, the way you are constituted with your specific gifts and your specific challenges, and how you are contextualized, in yourself, in your family, in your friends, in your work, in your spiritual life.

What is your Yes!? What are some of the key dimensions you want to pay attention to? Key perspectives or roles you have. You can start with three to five. What are the key roles that are critical to this big Yes! you have? Is your Yes! to be a great contributor, to be a great creator, to be fair? What is your Yes!? What are the different dimensions that you look at in your life of that Yes!? Is it in how you are in the work that you do for your inner development? In how you are a parent, how you live as a parent?

What are the major roles that you can start with? These are ways that you contribute towards your Big Yes! within each one of these different major roles in your life, what is important to you, and how does that contribute to your big Yes!? Here you are starting to look at defining your Big Yes!, your overall Yes!, in terms of the different roles. This helps describe the impacts of your Yes!, in terms of your own outcomes. What is it that each of these roles or perspectives in your life contributes to? A way of providing for the stability of your family that builds community and has an impact in life. Because of the excellent contribution you make, of what you do, to support the next generation in being their best, whatever that is. There are potential impacts. What is it for you? Your outcomes. Why is it that you do it? What is your Yes! that you bring to each of those different roles, that aligns with your big Yes!, your overall Yes!?

Next, look at some of the major time elements in your life. What are the three or four big buckets of things that you do that contribute towards that Yes!? Within that local perspective that is aligned with your big Yes!? These are your activities that drive your outputs. This is the big one. About one third of your day is spent sleeping. What is the quality of your sleep? How does it impact how strong you feel during the day? Your ability to show up for you? Maybe it is about eating. Your nutrition. The quality of your nutrition. Or is it about exercise? Or your inner development? Meditating, praying, doing exercise, yoga, stretching your body. What are the inner realms of your individual life that you bring to this? What is it in your work? What is it about your work and contribution that adds value to your Yes!? To your contribution?

What people tend to see, when describing these time segments, is that you now have about 40 hours per day of things that you need to do. The beauty of this is that you get 24 hours. So, now you can start to prioritize. Of these elements that are important, which ones are most critical to your big Yes!? These are critical roles that you have in your life. Like being a parent, working, and the inner work of taking care of yourself. Your relationship with the other, with the group, with your creative process, with nature and spirit. Given this, then how much time do each of these activities get? This is not about prioritizing our essential, life-giving activities, rather seeing how they fit and getting clear on how they contribute to your big Yes! With this clarity, you can fit them into your life activities.

You can look at this time element on a daily basis, on a weekly basis, on a monthly basis, on an annual basis. You might not do this activity every day, such as visiting with friends or taking a couple of hours to read a book or to do some painting, or to go on a long walk. That might be something that is more in the rhythm of the week, or the rhythm of the month. These things are critical to you to be able to make your contribution within this role. So maybe extending to a couple days of doing that, going on long hikes, going to meditation retreats, taking a class, or being with family and friends on an extended basis. Maybe it is on a monthly basis. Or maybe it is even an annual basis. You might need a break to go out to nature for a week every few months.

Look at what those time elements are, and start to add them up, for each of your roles. Add those up for your day. Your week, your month, your year. This is your hypothesis about your big Yes! These are the major contributing perspectives or roles that you have in contributing to your Yes! This is your strategy for them. These are the major activities that you have within each of these roles. Being your big Yes!, they need to happen. The question is about how you are going to fit them into your life. In a way that generates health and beauty.

In our years of working with this big Yes! exercise, we tend to find that you think you know what your big Yes! is, and then "life takes over," and you discover months or years later that you have said No! to most of your Yeses!. You have accepted the scarcity, the lack, the No! to your creativity. What you are doing with the big Yes! scorecard is aligning your big Yes! operating system, your agreements field. You are declaring that this is your big Yes! This is your organizing principle. These are the major contributions you have towards that organizing principle. These are the activities that you say Yes! to.

Within those activities of your Yes!, you can strengthen your ability to achieve that local-role perspective contribution to the Yes! Now how do you fit those in, if you initially listed forty hours of activities per day? You need to start seeing which ones lead to you getting stronger—greater health and beauty. Not seeing these as trade-offs. When you see them as trade-offs, you say, "I would like to do that, but I do not have the time. Therefore, I do not do it."

You want to exercise, but you do not. You want to read that book, but you do not. You want to visit your friends; you do not have the time. And it is part of your big Yes! If it is part of your Yes!, within these roles, then it is critical to make the time. The question then becomes what is part of your big Yes!? What are the roles that you say Yes! to? If it is not in your big Yes!, it is in your No! You are not going to do that. It is not designed into your operating system. Does that mean that it is permanently in your No!? No. You are working with your Yes! operating system to see and adjust. To evolve. To align your reality with your Yes! That is the point. See what happens with this Yes! Consciously choosing what you say Yes! to. Consciously paying attention to the feedback of what happens when you do, so that you can adjust and learn over time. You can change what you saw, what you are doing, what you are measuring. The impact. The outcome of those actions. This is your ability to start testing your strategy and adjusting, evolving.

BIG YES! SCORECARDS FOR INDIVIDUALS

Here are two brief examples of Big YES! scorecards. Mine and my friend Jay's. Both of these have evolved over time. They each reflect what we are seeing right now.

My Big YES! Scorecard

I will start with the key ingredients of my Big YES! scorecard. I want it to include my deeper shared purpose, the key roles I take on in my life that contribute to my deeper shared purpose, and guidance in prioritizing where I spend my time, my effort, in supporting each of those roles. As I look at the operating system that is my life, does it help me align with my Big YES!? By putting these elements together into one scorecard, I am able to see the difference between my desired system and priorities and those that I actually have. By seeing this more consciously, I can choose to adjust it.

Back in 2016, I developed my first Strategic Scorecard (Figure 10). As I worked through the main elements, I was able to see key elements of my Big YES! all on the same page. As I played with what elements to include and how to put them together on the page, I was able to see missing elements or redundancies, which had not been explicitly visible before I started. How do I know that? Because I did not include them in the first pass. They became visible when I started to see the whole.

2016 Strategic Scorecard

sustainable vibrancy is a choice

Realizing Self-supported Growth
thru black-swan optionality

Being   *Doing*   *Structuring*

Insights (ISC)
- Develop foundational frameworks & tools
  - Developing higher level seen thru 4 lenses
  - *Agreements* book, SAVE money
  - Taking the half-invented into the invented
- Build global abund-based research network
  - GI_MEDIR
- Certification
  - Standards
  - Verification process and platform
  - Delivery
    - Individuals – cohorts
    - Groups – Impact Resilience
- Realize sustainable funding
  - 3-years funding committed

Vibrancy
- Catalyze global social impact
  - Coordination
    - Lead university alliance
    - Certification
    - vNetwork structure
    - Platform
- Engage inter-locking self-funding growth
  - TJ project vinvite and admin processes

Family
- Support each other
  - Vibrancy is a choice in every moment
  - Monthly dates
- Strengthen self
  - Daily ritual space
  - Lift own body weight
- Establish foundations of sustainable funding
  - Bucket #1 met
  - Bucket #2 basic debt gone
  - Bucket #3 1x (B#1) supplemental income
  - Bucket #4 big-ticket items

Academy
- Live the curriculum
  - 75% participants from community
  - Full basic curriculum delivered by others
- Self-Aware Authentic Wellness
  - Establish foundations
  - Support initial efforts – experience, research, outreach
- THORLO
  - Support CUL growth
  - On-board TPG with CUL

Figure 10: JLRD 2016 Big Yes! Scorecard

The whole included my deeper shared purpose, which I phrased in 2016 as seeing that sustainable vibrancy is a choice, in everything I do, and that it is critical to support me in realizing self-supported growth for me and the organizations I lead. This means that they are able to generate the resources they need to grow. When looking at the big roles I was playing in my life at the time, I had my family, the research non-profit I led, my role in a foundation I led, and the consultancy I led.

I then looked at the major activities in each of these roles that depended critically on me. I iterated multiple times through this list, coming up also with a short list of goals for each major activity. This list of roles, major activities, and goals helped me begin to see a fuller picture of what I was doing and what was needed for achieving my purpose. With this framing of what I was doing in my roles towards my purpose, I could then begin to see how my time allocation to these activities aligned with my desired reality (Figure 11).

Time Allocation
sustainable vibrancy is a choice

Realizing Self-supported Growth
thru black-swan optionality

Being   *Doing*   *Structuring*

10d/mo
Insights (ISC)
3d/mo • Develop foundational frameworks & tools
Developing higher level seen thru 4 lenses
Agreements book, SAVE money
Taking the half-invented into the invented
3d/mo • Build global abund-based research network
GI_MEDIR
• Certification
1d/mo Standards
Verification process and platform
3d/mo Delivery
Individuals – cohorts
Groups – Impact Resilience
• Realize sustainable funding
3-years funding committed

6d/mo
Vibrancy
• Catalyze global social impact
4d/mo Coordination
Lead university alliance
Certification
vNetwork structure
Platform
• Engage inter-locking self-funding growth
2d/mo TJ project vinvite and admin processes

4h/d
Family
• Support each other
Vibrancy is a choice in every moment
Monthly dates
• Strengthen self
Daily ritual space
Lift own body weight
• Establish foundations of sustainable funding
Bucket #1 met
Bucket #2 basic debt gone
Bucket #3 1x (B#1) supplemental income
Bucket #4 big-ticket items

5d/mo
Academy
• Live the curriculum
75% participants from community
Full basic curriculum delivered by others
• Self-Aware Authentic Wellness
Establish foundations
Support initial efforts – experience, research, outreach
• THORLO
Support CUL growth
On-board TPG with CUL

Figure 11: JLRD Time Allocation in 2016 Big Yes! Scorecard

As I worked through the time allocations, I found two things. I started by writing down the amount of time I thought I should spend on each activity. Oops! The total added up to twice as much time as was available. Then I decided to look at the percentage of time I would dedicate to each major role in a given month. I started to align this with what those roles meant towards the emerging sense of my deeper shared purpose. Those role-level allocations gave me the amount of time available to work on each role in each month. I then started to allocate those role-level time allotments to the major activities. These numbers were far less than I had initially thought I needed to put to them. When I took a step back to look at the whole of the roles, the major activities, and time commitments, I started to imagine what it would be like to live into that life. It was quite different than my reality at that time. It felt good. It felt more aligned with what I wanted, as described by my emerging purpose, and with what I knew I could contribute to that purpose. I then started to organize my next weeks to see what it would feel like to live into this Big Yes!

The scorecard evolved over the next weeks. I played with the amount of time given to each role, and what that said for its priority in my Yes! I played with the amount of time I wanted to spend on each of the major activities and what they actually took. This led to continuous adjustments. This also led to questions about what agreements I needed to shift to be able to live into this new set of agreements with myself and with the communities I led. This was the start of another trip around the Agile Vibrancy Move Process, which we explored earlier in the book. As I found new agreements that better supported my ability to live into this scorecard, I found myself aligning more clearly, closely, and coherently with my Big Yes! And I found that my Big Yes! was evolving.

Another of couple iterations of my Big YES! scorecard led to my 2020 scorecard (Figure 12). In this scorecard, I focused on three levels of my work, from the core of all my work, the foundations that supported that core, and outreach needed to support those foundations. This involved roles of teaching, research, writing, and fieldwork.

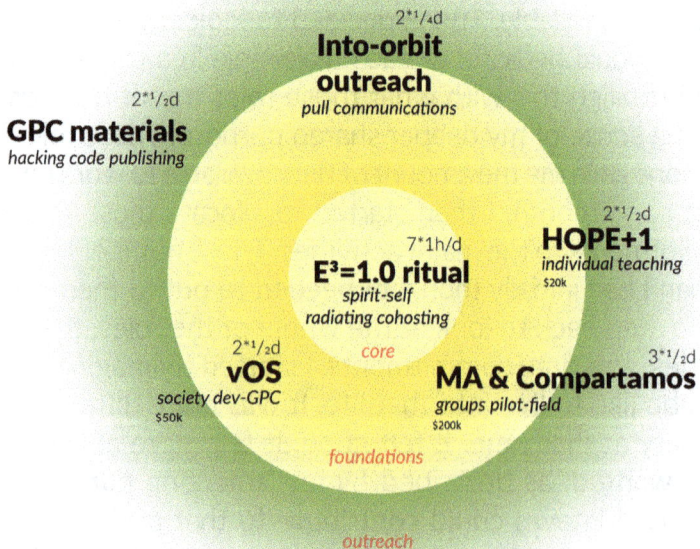

Figure 12: JLRD 2020 Big YES! Scorecard

Jay's Big YES! Scorecard

My friend Jay has also been working with his Big YES! Scorecard for a few years now. Here is what his looks like now, and how he describes the way he uses it.

"My Yes! is a way of defining the scope of what and how I choose to give my love and attention to. I have codified my Yes! into a graphic scorecard that I use as a reference to remind me of my center of gravity regardless of what circumstances I experience throughout the day. Stated differently, it supports me in not collapsing into something that is not consistent with my Yes!

The way I use my scorecard is threefold. The first is I use it as part of my morning meditation, to explicitly presence my Yes! at the beginning of my day. The second way that I use my scorecard is to interpret my experience during the day. A large part of how I experience my world is through feelings that are generated within my body. I use the scorecard to help interpret these feelings. For example, if I'm having an experience or anticipating an experience and that creates feelings of stress or of being off balance, like headaches, etc., I use my scorecard as a framework to evaluate how whatever that experience is or my anticipated experience is might be part of my Yes! or not. That creates a framework to help me explicitly say Yes! to continuing down that path or to helping me figure out how it is not part of that path. The third way that I use my scorecard is really a change-over-time metric. I compare earlier scorecards to my current scorecard to see if there is any change in awareness or identified things that are important to me now that were not in the past."

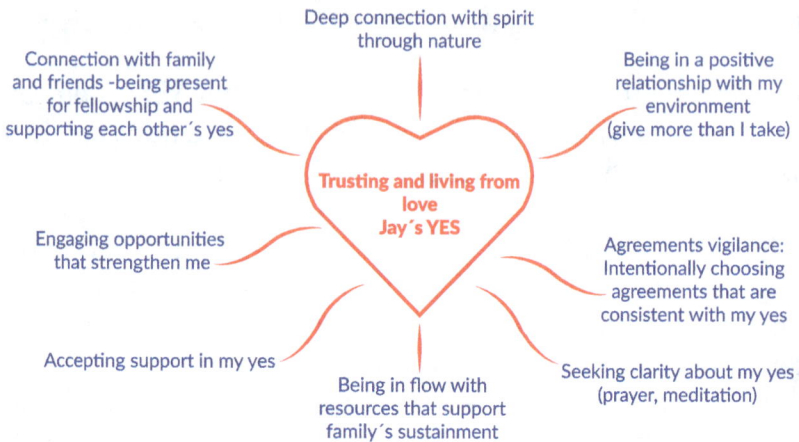

Deep connection with spirit through nature

Connection with family and friends -being present for fellowship and supporting each other's yes

Being in a positive relationship with my environment (give more than I take)

Trusting and living from love
Jay's YES

Engaging opportunities that strengthen me

Agreements vigilance: Intentionally choosing agreements that are consistent with my yes

Accepting support in my yes

Being in flow with resources that support family's sustainment

Seeking clarity about my yes (prayer, meditation)

Figure 13: Jay's Big Yes! Scorecard

BIG YES! SCORECARDS FOR GROUPS

Just as you can do an agreements field mapping of your big Yes! operating system for yourself, you can also do it for a group. Whether it is a team, a few people, an organization of multiple teams and functional areas, a system of supply chains of organizations that are coming together, a network, or a whole ecosystem of different organizations and communities working together on something. At each of these levels, you can map the operating system of your Big YES!

The group process for mapping out its operating system is very similar to the process for yourself. You start with the organizing principle, the deeper shared purpose. What is the purpose that you are organizing towards? What are the different perspectives needed? What do each of these perspectives bring to the game? What can you make real of that? What can you each commit to do to make that real? What is yours to contribute? What are the actions that you can take? These are the steps described in the O Process, which we saw back in Figure 6.

For example, let's look at a school. Whose perspectives are needed on the deeper shared purpose? It is an educational system, and you are the parents, and they are the kids, the teachers, the administrators, the people to take care of the building, the people who feed you, the people who clean your buildings and maintain the body of your school, its grounds and facilities. You need all of these different perspectives to come together. Who funds the schools? Is that public funding? You need government officials, the tax officials, the money people who are working to provide that money. The market, private investors, the families that are putting the money together. Somebody is administering. What are all the perspectives that are needed? What are they each trying to do? Where are they contributing? How do all these pieces fit together, to do what for the system? What does the feedback look like?

You can do this at the level of a group of people. As I described in an earlier book, *Ecosynomics: The Science of Abundance*, we used the O Process with many teams in a textile mill. We would start by getting clear on the group's purpose. We would make sure we could connect the group's "local purpose" with the company's deeper shared purpose. If this is who we serve as a company, what is this group's specific contribution, their specific purpose within the larger purpose?

Whose perspectives are needed to see the fullness of that specific purpose? For example, we had a team focused on integrating the marketing and sales ends of the business with the operations and production part of the business. The people who sell the product with the people who make it. This was a weekly coordination meeting across the company. The specific purpose of the meeting was to make sure that each end of the business was aligned with the other. As they prepared for the weekly meeting, the team's leaders would look at who needed to be in the room for the meeting. Whose perspectives are required? We know we need representatives from sales and marketing, as well as from operations and production. They are the meeting regulars, who integrate across the company. Given the specific topics for this coming week, do we have all of the necessary perspectives? If we are looking at accounting numbers or information systems, maybe we need to invite someone from those specific groups to attend. Following the O Process, this group also developed its capacity to efficiently surface the issues each group saw as critical for any given issue, then collectively integrate these perspectives into a shared understanding and how they each needed to commit to contributing to it. This meant that they developed the capacity to ask questions of each other. To know what the others could see that was different from what they could see. To know how to hold each other to their own standards of excellence. They also learned how to see a greater whole by integrating these different perspectives.

Now, how do you implement the scorecard for your big Yes!? The O Process helps you align your deeper shared purpose with the different perspectives on what is happening and what needs to happen to realize your purpose. In working with your Big Yes! scorecard, you are also evolving what you are learning over time. Earlier in the book, you used the Agile Vibrancy Move (Figure 8) to show what needed to change in the operating system to be able to operate at the next level of agreements, the agreements that operate at the level of deeper shared purpose you want to make real.

Using the Agile Vibrancy Move Process, you looked at your purpose. What is your goal? What you are trying to do. Where are you in achieving your purpose versus where you need to be? Over what time horizon do you see that you need to shift that? This is the first step.

In the second step of the process, you look at the agreements at the next level. The level of outcomes, impacts, and engagement you need to achieve. What are people who are operating at the next level of Yes! doing? What do you notice? Observe them. What does the next level of your big Yes! look like, in activities?

The third step looks at what you are actually doing. So now that you see what others do, look at what you do. As part of what you were just looking at in your operating system. This is your operating system. This is what others look like. What they are doing in their outcomes, their outputs, their impacts. Their direct actions, their behaviors and process variables or activities are different. What is it that you notice? What is it that you are ready to start trying?

The fourth step then develops the action plan for making the shifts in your operating system and testing them to see what works and what you learn about what works and what does not work. You can think of this as prototyping. You have an idea, which you can test. See what happens and adjust.

For the next iteration of the Agile Vibrancy Move process, you can test a second prototype. Trying and paying attention, seeing what happens. You can do that now, within the operating system that you designed for yourself, with your big Yes! scorecard. Your impact-resilience scorecard.

What comes next? Through the Agile Vibrancy Move process, you are testing shifts in your agreements, shifts in your underlying assumptions, shifts in agreements that shift your activities, what you do. That shifts your activities, your outputs, and your impacts.

You get feedback. You start to notice a shift. You pay attention to the costs of scarcity, the costs of entropy. You start to notice that there are some things that are very expensive to do, because they take you away from your natural state. Your natural state is a big Yes! As you have been seeing, throughout this book, saying No! has a cost. The cost of shutting down that Yes!, of closing down the energy, shutting off the access to that incredible energy of thought, of feeling, of willing, of engaging with others, of making your unique contribution, of growing yourself, supporting another, and another supporting you, as you each contribute your best.

Learning with each other. Learning from the feedback. Changing what you see, evolving as you engage, transform, and transfer purposeful energy.

What is the cost of not doing this? What is the cost of accepting your No!? What is the cost that you can reduce, by taking on your Yes!? There is a direct benefit from reducing the scarcity. By not doing this work, you are accepting a major cost. The next chapter explores these different costs of scarcity. The costs of entropy, the costs of not engaging that creative energy in yourself, in others, in groups. The cost of not doing that is all over the place. You will discover that the orders of magnitude of this cost are huge. Saying No! to human creativity is saying No! to love. It turns out a No! is very, very expensive. Saying Yes! is not hard; it is easy, because it is your natural state.

CHAPTER 7

THE COSTS OF SCARCITY OF YOUR NO! OPERATING SYSTEM

With an impact value operating system, your big Yes! operating system, you can now begin to see the costs of scarcity, the costs of entropy. This is something that adds value. Something that gives you an argument for the benefit of doing this work. The investment is taking the time and effort to do it. To learn and evolve. About how you want to improve your own reality, your own system, your experience, your outcomes. Your outcomes, as the investment, if you want to see it that way.

The benefit is both increased output and increased impact. Being aligned with your big Yes! towards your big purpose, your service. As well as reduction of the massive costs of scarcity.

What are these costs of scarcity? One way to understand this is by looking at each of the nine dimensions of your agreements field, which you explored starting back in chapter 2.

Let's take a first pass at looking through each of these nine dimensions. What are some of the costs of scarcity that you can see within each? What are some of the ways that you can assess the level of these costs of scarcity that you have within each of these dimensions? This is the benefit you can achieve by shutting down that cost of scarcity, by saying Yes! instead of accepting the No!

You will see that the benefits of saying Yes! versus accepting the costs of scarcity and entropy are huge. Not a 10% increase in value experienced, rather a hundredfold or a thousandfold increase. That sounds good. Let's go find some for you.

Remember that the agreements field includes three major complementary elements of this big geometry. You engage the purposeful energy. You transform that energy into something else for others. You transfer that energy to others. Engaging, transforming, and transferring. Since it is one agreements field, you can start anywhere, as long as you move through all of the dimensions, to understand the full geometry of your agreements field. For example, knowing that, you can start with the dimension connection to purpose.

ENGAGING ENERGY

As you saw earlier, how you engage the energy of your agreements field has three dimensions: (1) connecting to purpose; (2) choosing how you are connected; and (3) generating the experience.

Connecting to Purpose

When you are looking at engaging energy, the first dimension of engaging asks whether you are actually plugged in, referred to technically as your Continuity Power (P_c). What percentage of the time do you remember to organize around your deeper shared purpose? Do you actually pay attention to it, and does it guide your work?

The deeper shared purpose. For now, you can look at connecting to purpose from three levels: low; medium; and high. What are the associated costs of scarcity or entropy at each level? What does that do to you? What is the order of magnitude of this? At a very low level, you experience that you rarely connect to the purpose. You might not even know what the purpose of the group is. It might be somebody else's purpose. You might be there because somebody tells you to show up, and you do. But you are not clear about the organizing principle. Even when it is written somewhere, if it is never enacted, it is not the guiding principle for what you are doing. It does not organize your thinking. You are not connected to the energy of that purpose.

One simple way to measure the level of connection is to ask what percentage of the time are people in the group even aware of the purpose. Is everyone aware of the same purpose? What percentage of the time, in this group, is that what guides you? If it is from zero to very low, what are the costs of scarcity, of entropy, that you experience? First of all, you probably find it even hard to get the right people in the room, because there is nothing that they are serving. It is not clear whose voices are needed. It is not clear what you are actually trying to do. There is no organizing principle. This is one of the bigger costs of scarcity. Being able to get the energy into the room, the people into the room who can connect to that. What is the cost of having the wrong people in the room? The cost of not having the right people in the room? What is the cost of not even knowing what you are connecting to? The cost is massive. What is the probability that you will be able to do something that will move what you are trying to do forward, if you do not know what it is, and you are not connected to it? The probability approximates zero. This is a massive cost of not knowing what you are trying to do, in the first place.

> **Take A Moment.** Think of a specific group that you experience being this way, not good at connecting to purpose. Write down three to four of these costs of scarcity that immediately come to you.

Now, look at a group where the connection to purpose is moderate. About half the time you are connected to purpose. You do know what you are doing. You do remember what you are here for. In these groups, you do remember, because it is written down. It is usually in some book, written somewhere, on some poster. People have learned that it is the mantra of your group. You remember to do that. You might even have processes for helping you remember. At the beginning of the meeting. You might have somebody whose role it is to be the process co-host, to help you come back to that purpose. You might have a facilitator that always reminds you. You might put it on the wall. It tends to be written down, and fairly consistent.

> **Take Another Moment.** Think of a specific group that you experience that connects to its purpose some of the time. Write down three to four costs of scarcity that immediately come to you.

One of the costs of scarcity here is in the ability to adjust. Shifting how you are serving this purpose. What you are learning about your purpose. These are the costs of not having that clarity, or of having it half of the time and not the other half. Are you able to attract people who are used to a very high-level of engagement and performance? If you cannot attract them into the room, are you able to really refine how you focus on all elements of what you are doing towards your purpose? If not, then the half of the time that you are not connected directly to the purpose, you are giving energy to a lot of other things. You are somewhat efficient and effective. You might function better than groups that do not even know what their purpose is. Maybe even orders of magnitude better, but you are still not always on purpose. Those things that take you off purpose can take a lot of energy out of the room. Maybe even massive amounts of energy; most of it. They can be very fatiguing.

> **Take Another Moment.** Think of a specific group that you experience that often connects to purpose. Write down three to four costs of scarcity that think of off the top of your head.

In groups that score very high on connecting to purpose, they are always attentive to centering on purpose. Whenever someone in the group feels like they are unclear how the current exploration is on purpose, two things happen. First, they start with the assumption that what is being shared is on purpose, they just cannot see it. Second, they ask. "Help me see how this is on purpose. I trust that it is. I cannot see it. Help me see it. If it is not on purpose, then we can get back on purpose. If it is on purpose, and I could not see it, now I can, with you." This process means you are learning. You are getting better, together. You are adjusting, evolving in our service to this purpose. How can you connect to your service better, over time? In this situation, the costs of scarcity are much lower than in the lower levels of connection to purpose.

> Take A Final Moment. Think of a specific group that you experience connecting deeply to purpose. Write down three to four of these costs of scarcity that immediately come to you.

Choosing how you are connected

You are connected to the purpose. How are you listening to the voices in the room? How are you cohosting the possibility? The agreements field dimension of choosing how you are connected, is technically called Co-hosting (C).

At the very low level of cohosting, you are not paying attention to the different kinds of awareness you have in the room, the kinds of contributions in the room, or how to bring out the best of what each is bringing. When the level of cohosting is very low, usually one person is talking over others. Everybody else contributes very little to nothing. Nobody is holding the space for why they need the other voices in the room. What are some of the costs of scarcity? The lack of ability to discern who is in the room. Nobody understands why these people are in the room, so there is no holding each other responsible to sharing. The quality of what is shared. The quantity of what is shared. The differences in perspectives. They are not needed, so they are not expressed, even though they are in the room. This is dangerous. The answer to what the group needed to know, to avoid a costly mistake was in the room, and it did not come out, because of the process.

Informal Survey. Another one of my informal surveys. When the group discovers a mistake, and someone says, "I could have told you that was going to happen," I ask my question. "Why didn't you say that back when it was discussed?" I have heard the same answer, in many different cultures. "You did not ask. There was no space to share what I saw. Nobody saw that my contribution in that moment was critical." This simple survey surfaces a deep dynamic that has major impacts on the group, a dynamic that is easy to shift.

> **Take A Moment.** Like you did before, think about a group where you have had this experience of a very low level of co-hosting. Without giving it much thought, what are three to four costs of scarcity you see?

Groups at the middle level of the ability to co-host are paying attention to whose voices are needed. They are clear on why they need each other. Whose voices and perspectives are needed. Like the earlier example with the engineer, marketer, and accountant. To know if this will work, you need to know how much it will cost you to make it, from the engineer, how much you can sell it for, from the marketing person, and whether you can make money doing that, from the accountant. You each know you need each other's perspective. At this middle level, you are learning with each other about how to be clear that you need these perspectives in the room.

The costs of scarcity at this level are that you still tend to focus on what you already know, your proven capacities, from your own perspective. What you are learning from your already-proven capacities. What it is that you are seeing for the group, from what you already know. The lack here is the lack of what is new. What is vulnerable in you that you do not yet know? The group does not yet support you in connecting to new things. This brings in the risk of being unable to attract people who are very comfortable in the creative aspects of trying something new. People who are able to learn and evolve. You are risking the ability to see the new that is emerging. You are also still unable to pay attention to the different ways of knowing that each person brings. This means you miss knowing who to ask what questions, in any given moment.

> **Take Another Moment.** Think about a group where you have had this experience of a moderate level of co-hosting. Off the top of your head, what are three to four costs of scarcity you see?

At a high level, you are aware of what each person brings. Who is best at connecting to the gross, subtle, and causal nature of what is happening? Who brings what unique gifts. You can start to learn how to listen to and from each perspective. What is being for you, with you, for each of you in the room. You can also start to hold the excellence of each other, for each other. What does excellence in you look like? Are you bringing your best game? Are you participating fully? Are you seeing what is new? Are you able to see more of what is new in perspectives or categories or information through your listening with another?

> **And Take Another Moment.** Think about a group where you have experienced a high level of co-hosting. From what you experienced, what are three to four costs of scarcity you see?

Generating the Experience

The third dimension or geometry of engaging the energy is the experience of the vibrancy available through the five primary relationships of self, other, group, nature, and spirit. Technically this is referred to as Experience (E_x). At the low level, you experience a low level of trust, of confidence that you can share what is being asked of you. At this low level of trust, you tend to share the already-known, from your proven capacities. What the group expects of you. What they see that you can bring. They have the people in the room who can do what is expected, with their given capacities. You know what is in the book of wisdom, which tells you how things work.

What are the costs of scarcity of this level of experience? Each individual is only bringing what they can prove they already know. No new outcomes, no new thinking, and definitely not new possibilities. You are shutting out most of the ability for people to contribute at a higher level. This makes it difficult to attract people who can bring this creativity and learning. This is the cost of scarcity of not being able to invite those learnings into the room. This group will inevitably be caught by many surprises.

> Take A Moment. Let yourself think about a group where you experienced a very low level of engaging. From what you remember of that experience, what are three to four costs of scarcity you see?

At the middle level of a medium vibrancy experienced, in this third dimension of engaging, groups are learning and adjusting over time. They are asking questions, listening to each other, supporting each other in their learning.

The costs of scarcity here are in the group's ability to see deep innovation, to really support each other, stretching into new areas. And while this is what the group knows, and this is what they have learned about what they already know, what is it they do not know yet? What is it they could try? What is the deeper creativity that they have available to them, the new capacities and relationships that could support them, if they could really trust to be really vulnerable in this group? The lack of that makes it difficult to attract people who are very good at deep learning, and that leads to obsolescence, again.

> Take A Moment. Reflect on a group where you experienced a somewhat engaging experience. From what you remember of that experience, what are three to four costs of scarcity you see?

At the high level of vibrancy experienced, groups are deeply engaged. With the support of the co-hosts, the group is able to pay attention to both the deeper shared purpose they are in service to, as well as to the insights coming into the room from each person's unique perspective. They listen for those perspectives, supporting those individuals in seeing and contributing their best, building off of each other. They look for the new insights, which they interweave with the received wisdom from their earlier experiences.

Take A Moment. Reflect on a group where you experienced a highly engaging experience. From what you remember of that experience, what are three to four costs of scarcity you see?

Seeing All 3 Dimensions of Engaging

With these three sub-geometries or dimensions of engaging, you have low, medium, and high levels. Our research and experience with thousands of groups shows that groups tend to experience a similar level on all three dimensions. Analysis shows that this is because they are three subdimensions of the one agreements field. The costs of scarcity of the low level of engaging are in not being able to engage that energy, not being able to engage people who are used to bringing that energy. At the medium level, groups are able to engage people who are able to learn and who can bring their objective capacities to the game. They are able to listen to them. At the highest level of engaging, groups know what capacities they need and what capacities they have. They know what excellence looks like in each other. The lower levels do not have this. This is the great cost of scarcity in engaging.

TRANSFORMING ENERGY

Now let's look at the costs of scarcity in your transforming energy dimensions. Here you saw three dimensions or geometries within transforming the energy your organization engaged. Your capacity to transform that energy into something else. Your ability to leverage the system. Your resilience in accessing the resources you need on a continuous basis.

Potential Energy

What are the costs of scarcity at different levels of the ability to connect the engaged energy? Technically this is referred to as the Potential Energy (E_P). The engaged energy is there. Now, can you connect to it? Can you access it to transform it? This is the way your organization is structured to work with outcomes or nouns, with activities and learning, with developing capacities and relationships over time, with potential and possibilities.

Groups where the ability to connect to the potential energy is low have organizational structures and processes that are very focused on outcome measurement. What actually happened. The outputs, and that is it. This is what you find. You refer constantly to the book. You know what you are supposed to measure, and that is it. When someone says, "I thought maybe we could...," they are immediately told, "There is no maybe. Just do what is in the book."

The costs of scarcity here are everything that you would be able to do if you could engage at higher levels, because you are not connecting to it. You do not have any place to do anything with it. People experience this as very frustrating and disengaging. Even when you ask someone a question, and they share what they are learning, in the meeting, nothing ever happens. Nothing can result from learning at the low level of agreements.

> **Take A Moment.** Remember a group where you experienced a low level of the ability to connect to the potential energy. From what you remember, what are three to four costs of scarcity you see?

At the medium level of potential energy, groups have organizational structures and processes that support learning and development of relationships and capacities over time. You have mentors. You ask questions in group meetings, and they listen. You look at what you learned, at what you said you were going to learn, at what you actually learned, from going and doing something. You spend time on that. You have learning libraries. You have ways of capturing lessons learned over time.

The costs of scarcity here are in assuming that you still know what you are supposed to be measuring. Measuring in ways to continue within the existing system. The costs of scarcity at the medium level are the inability to connect to what is emerging, the new, the ability to bring in the exciting and innovative. The ability to engage people who are paying attention to and dealing with the emerging reality. Giving the space and time for it.

> **Take Another Moment.** Think about a group where you experienced a medium level of the ability to connect to the potential energy. Reconnecting to that experience, what are three to four costs of scarcity you see?

At the high level of potential energy, the costs of scarcity are very low. You are paying attention to all the resources that you have, to what you are able to see towards the future, what you are learning over time, and the outcomes that you are achieving. Working with the assets that support your innovating, your learning and developing outcomes. You make decisions based on this. You have structures that support making the decisions you need to make, for yourself. You support each other in the contributions you each make to the group, and how the group supports each other's creative process for seeing something new, seeing a pathway to getting the feedback, and to learning and adjusting over time. Working with the creativity that is everywhere, in what you perceive from the past, and what you are learning right now, and what you can begin to see in each member of the group, in what you each contribute towards the shared purpose.

> **Take A Final Moment.** Think about a group where you experienced a high level of the ability to connect to the potential energy. Reconnecting to that experience, what are three to four costs of scarcity you see?

Systemic Leverage

The second dimension of transforming energy is Systemic Leverage, technically (Lsys). Groups at a very low level of systemic leverage have very low direct, dynamic, and structural leverage. They are not efficient or effective in their direct actions. They do not understand the dynamics of how their area of contribution works. This results in continuously fighting against the dynamics of the system. They are not coordinating efforts across these different mechanisms. Their costs of scarcity include having inputs that lead to very low outputs, leading to huge losses of energy and inefficiencies.

> Take A Moment. Think about a group where you experienced a low level of systemic leverage. Immersing yourself in that experience, what three to four costs of scarcity do you see?

At the moderate level of systemic leverage, groups are more experienced, being quite effective and efficient at the direct level of your actions. The things you do result in high-quality outputs for your inputs. You know what you are doing professionally. You might even be best-in-class or at least at the level of operational excellence. You meet a high benchmark, a high standard in your direct actions. You tend to have people who have wisdom in the area and understand the dynamics of their area, so you are not fighting the system's dynamics. You are working with the inertia of the system. You have some capacity to coordinate and pool efforts from across these dynamics. The costs of scarcity here are in not understanding completely the different dynamics of each area, as they change over time. You might be fighting the system, when all of a sudden it begins to move directly with you. You often do not recognize this shift in time. You might have been in a building phase of the dynamics—it was strengthening and then began to accelerate—and now a balancing or homeostasis mechanism is coming into place.

The costs of scarcity are in not recognizing the difference, the shifting. At this level, the group is also not very good at coordinating across the shifting of these dynamics. These are huge costs of scarcity.

> Take A Moment. Remember a group where you experienced a medium level of systemic leverage. Putting yourself in the experience of that group, what three to four costs of scarcity do you see?

At the high level of systemic leverage, groups are very efficient at what they do with their direct actions. You understand and work on continuously evolving your understanding of the dynamics that exist and are emerging within each of your areas. You work to coordinate that these different dynamics, within each of the different areas, are generating the overall outcome that you wish, together. You are coordinating systemically across these influencing dynamics, and the actions you are taking within the system to leverage. The costs of scarcity are very low.

> Take A Moment. Think about a group where you experienced a high level of systemic leverage. What three to four costs of scarcity do you see?

Resilience

The third dimension or geometry within transforming energy is Resilience, technically (R_{DES}). At a low level of resilience, your group does not have access to the resources that you need to do your work. You are always begging for resources. You might have access to one source, depending on the whims of that single source.

The costs of scarcity come from having to spend massive amounts of effort and stress in getting the resources, and not on using the resources. They spend lots of time fretting about how to get access to the resources.

> Take A Moment. Think about a group where you experienced low resilience. Remembering that experience, what three to four costs of scarcity do you see?

At the middle level of resilience, groups have access to multiple sources of the required resources. You are aware of the dynamics. You are aware of what is coming and what is going. You are able to shift amongst the resources that you have access to, as well as how you access them. You might even be aware of some of the rhythms, in the time of the year, or in a specific part of a cycle. You focus on these sources, to be able to work with that. The difficulty here is in still being dependent.

The costs of scarcity here are that you are still dependent on others to provide the resources you need, even if you understand the dynamics.

> **Take A Moment.** Go back to your memory of a group where you experienced a middle level of resilience. Remembering that experience, what three to four costs of scarcity do you see?

At the high level of resilience, your group is able to work with the input of resources that you are accessing from others, and you generate many of the resources you need for yourself. You have your own resources, and you have multiple ways of generating the resources you need. You understand the rhythms and cycles of those. You welcome the input of other's resources as vital nutrients to shifting how you think about things. You are able to evolve, without depending entirely on access to the resources of others.

> **Take A Moment.** Think about a group where you experienced high resilience. What three to four costs of scarcity do you see?

Seeing All 3 Dimensions of Transforming

These three sub-geometries or dimensions of transforming also express as low, medium, and high levels. Like with the three dimensions of engaging, groups tend to experience a similar level on all three dimensions of transforming. This is because they are also three subdimensions of the same agreements field. The costs of scarcity of the low level of transforming are in not knowing how to connect to, work with, or support the levels of the engaged energy. At the medium level of transforming, groups are able to connect to the engaged energy, learn and develop over time, knowing how to leverage resource inputs into outputs that drive value for others, with sufficient resilience in resources. At the highest level of transforming, groups connect with the full potential of highly engaged energy, very efficiently and effectively leveraging resource inputs into high-value outputs, with the capacity to regenerate the resources that sustain their work. That the lower levels cannot do this is their great cost of scarcity in transforming.

TRANSFERRING ENERGY

The third area in the agreements field is the transfer of that energy. The three sub-geometries of transferring are (1) network virality—do the intended recipients of the transformed energy want it and can they receive it in the form it is offered, (2) what impact are you actually offering them, and (3) who is invited and involved—everyone everywhere everyday.

Network Virality

The first dimension of transferring energy is Network Virality, technically (N). The question here is whether others in the network of your ecosystem will take up what you offer.

At the low level of network virality, the intended recipients are not engaged. They do not want what your group is offering, and they are not able to receive it in the form that you are offering it.

The costs of scarcity. Your group puts energy into engaging and transforming. When you transfer energy at a low level, where the intended recipients do not really want your offer —they do not value it— your group is at a high risk of not receiving the resources it needs to be able to do this work in the first place.

> Take A Moment. Think about a group where you experienced low network virality—the intended recipients did not want what you were offering them. What three to four costs of scarcity do you see?

At the medium level of network virality, you are engaging the intended recipients. Usually, the intended recipients are quite engaged. They more or less want what your group is offering, and they give your group feedback on it. They are talking with you, often working side-by-side with you. Sometimes the intended recipients can receive what you offer in the form that you are offering it.

The costs of scarcity here are that, while the recipients are engaged, your group does not really know what they really want. While you are interacting with the intended recipients, your group is still working from its own perspective, so you do not really know what the intended recipients deeply value and you do not know how those values are shifting over time. So you are still at risk, in the future, of not being able to adjust with your intended recipients, in what they want and in what you are offering. It might work some of the time, in some of the ways. You are not reaching your full potential. You are not deeply understanding what your intended recipients want.

> **Take A Moment.** Think about a group where you experienced medium network virality. What three to four costs of scarcity do you see?

At the high level of network virality, your intended recipients deeply engage with you. Your group knows that the intended recipients want what you are offering because you are designing it with them, adjusting with them, over time. You know that they want what you are offering, and they are able to receive it in the form in which it is being offered.

> **Take A Moment.** Remember a group where you experienced high network virality. Putting yourself in a specific experience with that group, what three to four costs of scarcity do you see?

Global Goal

The second element of transferring energy is the Global Goal, the organizing principle, the purpose of this effort. This is the purpose that people are connecting to in the engaging energy, technically (Y_{GG}).

At a low level of purpose, your group does not really know why it is organized, what it is trying to do. In this situation, the probability of achieving the purpose is very low.

The costs of scarcity are in missing the mark. Not being able to transfer the transformed energy, because you do not know what you are transferring.

> Take A Moment. Remember a group where you experienced a low level of purpose. Thinking about a specific experience with that group, what three to four costs of scarcity do you see?

At a medium level of purpose, your group is pretty clear on the purpose. You are not necessarily meeting your purpose, but you are working towards it. You might not be shifting how you are able to work towards it, but you are learning and developing.

The costs of scarcity are your inability to really meet this purpose. You are not able to engage the people that are here to be really met. You are missing a clear definition of what you are really here to do.

> Take A Moment. Remember a group where you experienced a medium level of purpose. Thinking about a specific experience with that group, what three to four costs of scarcity do you see?

At a high level of purpose, your group is very clear on its purpose. While you are making significant strides, continuously, in service to your purpose, you are always stretching what you understand of your purpose. You are evolving as you learn more about your purpose, along the way.

> Take A Moment. Remember a group where you experienced a high level of purpose. What three to four costs of scarcity do you see?

Everyone Everywhere Everyday (E³)

The third dimension of transferring energy is who is invited and involved in your conscious ecosystem, technically referred to as your ability to reach everyone, everywhere, everyday, pronounced "eCubed" (E³).

When E^3 is very low, that means your group is only serving some of the people in some of the geographies of the system that you said you intended to serve. You are only serving some of them some of the time. So, while you might be engaged, you might be transforming the energy, and your intended recipients might even want what you offer, but who is the "they" that wants it and is your group serving them? Is your group able to achieve serving everyone, within any of the geographies? How many geographies are you able to serve? What percentage of the time? As that purpose extends out, over space and over time, what is that impact?

The costs of scarcity of a low E^3 are in the lack of demand for what you are offering, and in the lack of clarity of who you are really serving. You said, in your purpose, that you had organized your system to serve a specific group of people, yet you are not.

> Take A Moment. Remember a group where you experienced low E^3. What three to four costs of scarcity do you see?

At a moderate level of E^3, your group is serving a subset of the intended people within certain geographies, a good chunk of the time. You are learning and developing your capacity to serve more of them.

The costs of scarcity are some deep structures. Your systems are not designed to reach certain geographies of your intended recipients, often for deep structural reasons. So, even if you try to reach them, you cannot, running into deep inefficiencies and the experience of ineffectiveness in serving specific communities of intended recipients.

> Take A Moment. Remember a group where you experienced medium E^3. What three to four costs of scarcity do you see?

Serving everyone, within all the geographies, all of the time (E^3) at a high level means that everyone is being served by the system. They are deeply engaged, in all demographics. Your group has figured out what that means, in different contexts, as they are constituted differently, in different groups of people, with different characteristics, throughout the system. You are continuously engaged. The system deeply works for all intended recipients. Your group is continuously able to evolve, continuously serving and learning, as one ecosystem together.

Take A Moment. Remember a group where you experienced high E^3. What three to four costs of scarcity do you see?

Seeing All 3 Dimensions of Transferring

The three sub-geometries or dimensions of transferring express at low, medium, and high levels. Like with the three dimensions of engaging and transforming, groups tend to experience a similar level on all three dimensions of transferring. Again, this is because these are also three subdimensions of the same agreements field. The costs of scarcity of a low level of transferring are in not knowing and being able to serve the actual reality of your intended recipients. At the medium level of transferring, your group works with the intended recipients and is able to transfer the transformed energy to many of them much of the time. At the highest level of transferring, your group works deeply and continuously with the intended recipients, evolving your understanding of what to offer and how to break down structural barriers to serving all of your intended recipients all of the time. The lower levels of transferring cannot do this, and that is their great cost of scarcity in transferring.

INTEGRATING THE ENGAGING, TRANSFORMING, AND TRANSFERRING ENERGIES

Pulling all this together, with the costs of scarcity—the costs of entropy—in engaging, transforming, and transferring this energy, you see that when the level of this energy of the agreements field is low, in your ability to engage, your ability to transform, and your ability to transfer, the costs of scarcity are very high. The risk of obsolescence is extraordinary. You do not know what resources you have. As things shift in the system, the probability that you will get caught by surprise and without is very high. You are not able to attract the people who want to play. Learning and developing is hard. You are not able to attract the people who are efficient and effective at doing what you want within your system.

It is hard to get out of the deep scarcity of the weak agreements field. The high costs of scarcity of shutting people down, of saying No! to human creativity. No! to connection to purpose, to listening to their voices, to trust, to knowing how to work with what the group is learning. With what you bring, with what you are learning, with new insights, with knowing how to transform that into things that people value and want to engage with and can receive in all forms. For everyone everywhere everyday, on a resilient basis. The low level of the agreements field is missing all of that.

> **Take A Moment.** Looking back at your reflections, on your experience of low levels of each of the nine dimensions of your agreements field, put them all together now. These are your first pass at the costs of scarcity of your weak agreements fields. What do you see?

At the moderate strength of your agreements field, you see that you can engage people. People are in service and learning, bringing their best capacities. They are learning and working together, cooperating, transforming the energies somewhat efficiently and effectively, in ways that serve many of the people in the system much of the time.

The costs of scarcity are in the inability to bring out the best contributions of your group, to bring out the best in the intended recipients and their deeper needs, and in the inability to evolve your purpose and your service to that purpose.

> **Take A Moment.** Look back at your reflections on your experience of medium levels of each of the nine dimensions of your agreements field. Pull all of them all together. These are your first pass at the costs of scarcity of your moderate agreements fields. What does this show you?

With your strong agreements fields, you are able to take advantage of what is emerging, what you are learning, and what you can each bring. How you engage the best of who you are, with each other, and step further into the best of you are. What you can each contribute, as you engage, transform, and transfer.

Take A Moment. Look at your reflections on your experience of high levels of each of the nine dimensions of your agreements field. These are your first pass at the costs of scarcity of your strong agreements fields. What do you see?

This brings you back to your natural state. The state of high connection. You know how to do this. It is part of who you are as beings of light, as *Homo lumens*. You are capable of doing this. This is your natural state. Doing any less, at lower levels of the agreements field, is saying No!. It is accepting a No! This is your No! scorecard. That No! scorecard has costs. These costs are not insignificant. They are huge. Another way of saying this is, if you accept that No!, what is normal is the current state of disengagement, in turning out the light, saying No! to human creativity, believing this state is normal. Doing those other things, the Yeses!, would be nice, and maybe they could lead to some impact.

Framing it in the other way, saying Yes! is normal. It is your ordinary state. The extraordinary state—the not ordinary state—is saying No! The cost of doing so is huge. Those who are saying Yes! do not have those massive costs of scarcity. They have great benefits and very low costs.

People who say No! to all of this have very weak agreements field. They do not get the benefits, and they have huge costs of scarcity.

Take One Last Moment. Look at your reflections on your experience of weak, moderate, and strong agreements field. This shows you that you have different experiences, and that stronger experiences are available to you. What do you see that differentiates your weak, moderate, and strong agreements fields? How do they feel different? What is the difference in their impact? This is the first step towards choosing the strength of the agreements field you consciously accept.

This brings us all the way back to the beginning, when we said you start with a Yes! The benefits are huge, and the costs are low. Even if you are unconscious of what you are doing, when you start with a Yes!, and you live with a Yes!, then what we have discovered is that the net results, the outputs and impacts, are always net positive. The benefits far exceed the costs. We discovered that when you start with a No!, when you accept weak agreements fields, then you have very weak benefits from all of the work that people are putting into the systems, from all those calories that they are expending. The benefits are weak, and the costs of scarcity are huge.

No matter what you do, no matter how hard you try, if you start with a No!, and you align around a No! scorecard, the net result is always negative. Massively negative. We then come back to the choice. Do you prefer Yes! or No!? If you say Yes!, and you align around your Yes!, the benefits are always net positive. Far more value is generated. If you start with a No!, the effect is always net negative. It is your choice.

Diving deeper -- calibrating what you see

This is your perspective. You can add more evidence. You can add other perspectives. With these additions, you can robustly calibrate your own perception. You can invite the dimensions of an experience that others perceive, that you might miss. You can invite their support in shifting the agreements. There are many tools for supporting a deeper dive. Some have been shared here. You can find others at the Institute for Strategic Clarity (isclarity.org) and my blog (jlrd.me).

CONNECTING WITH LOWER-ENGAGEMENT LEADERS

What do you do if you have to work with leaders of low-engagement groups? Think about how you make sense of your world, and how they make sense of their world.

Your way of making sense of the world is clearly useful. It seems to work for you. You got this far. Then you meet people who just do not see the world as clearly as you do. They seem to see it differently. While there are many explanations for differences in worldview (different cultures, different languages, different life experiences), one difference we have found to be critical is in what you perceive to be real. Your level of perceived reality.

Do you tend to see reality as that which you can touch? Mostly it is what is directly right here right now, often in quite material terms. That is real. Or do you also include how things ebb and flow over time, how people develop in new capacities and relationships? It is about the material and the dynamics of networks of influence. That is real. Or do you also include the potential you and others see in what is not yet here, in the creative arts? It is about the outcomes and the learning and the potential. That is real. Or do you also include the learning from feedback of what actually happens, and how that informs the potential you see, in service to a deeper purpose, and pathways to getting there. It is about evolutionary co-tangibilizing. That is real. It turns out that these are four very different perspectives of what is real. And most people think that theirs is the right and only one, in any given moment. At each of these four levels, you are adding dimensions of reality.

The Institute for Strategic Clarity's global survey research, with over 196,000 people from 126 countries, finds that there is a distribution of people, across these four perspectives of what is real. And, the same people might vary what they perceive to be real depending on the group they are with, the group's **agreements field**–how the group engages, transforms, and transfers creative energy.

Communicating with someone who is working with a different perspective of what is real, along this continuum, is very challenging. If you perceive more of reality to exist than they do, they don't necessarily see you as stronger, rather weaker. That their reality doesn't include dimensions that yours does means that you are focusing on things that are invisible or irrelevant to them. Those dimensions you find to be so interesting are not in their equation.

Here is a 4-step process to communicating with someone with a different perspective of what is real.

Step #1 — Where You Are

The first step to communicating with someone with a different perspective of what is real is to determine where you are, what you include in your perspective of reality. In very simple terms, you can think of these as nouns-only, verbs-nouns, light-verbs-nouns, and ecosystems of sacred hospitality levels of reality.

- Nouns-only — there are things, mostly material, that are right here right now

- Verb-nouns — there are things, and there is change over time and space

- Light-verbs-nouns — there are things, change, and always-present creative potential

- Ecosystems of sacred hospitality — there are things, change, creative potential, all in an ever-evolving service to a deeper shared purpose

Step #2 — Where They Are

The second step is to determine where they are. How does the person you are communicating with see the world? What do they include in what they perceive to be real?

Step #3 — Understand How They See You from Their Reality

The other person can only see you and your reality from their reality. If your reality has more dimensions than theirs, they don't see that. Often your attention to and inclusion of these other dimensions creates confusion for them. You are talking about things that are not in their definition of what is real, which usually is interpreted by them as a weakness. What you are going on and on about isn't real.

The following table provides a first scan of what each perspective of reality experiences when communicating with someone from one of the other perspectives. This is based on what we observe when working with people across levels.

Perceived Reality	N Sees	VN Sees	LVN Sees	ESH Sees
Ecosystems of Sacred Hospitality (ESH)	High-risk explorers	Lack of alignment on agreed purpose	Shifting purpose	Comprehensive clarity (purposeful evolution)
Light-Verbs-Nouns (LVN)	Lack of clear focus (high risk ventures)	Lack of applying learnings	Comprehensive clarity (tangibilization)	Beingness
Verbs-Nouns (VN)	Inefficient, always experimenting	Comprehensive clarity (learning)	Stuck in own thinking	Becoming
Noun-only (N)	Comprehensive clarity (efficiency)	Static surprise from dynamics	Collapsed in outcomes	Already finished

Table 3: Levels of Perceived Reality in Communicating with Others

If they are coming from a perspective with fewer dimensions of perceived reality than you–for example, they see Nouns-only (N), and you see Verbs-Nouns (VN)–they see your focus on learning and developing new capacities and relationships as being inefficient. You are always experimenting with something new, never focused on what you have already done. Always moving on to the next thing and not leveraging what you already have.

Step #4 — How to Communicate with Them

To communicate with them, you are trying to invite them into a reality, yours, that is not part of their reality. It works best to start with remembering what they see as real. If you are a Verb-Noun reality person, you might be most excited about sharing your focus on the learning, the verbs. To you the importance of the nouns is obvious and already proven, so you are focused on how to improve on what you already know. To communicate with the Nouns-only person, start by showing that you can speak their language, in their reality. Yes, you have nouns, which you have proven to be efficient. You have outcomes. You are efficient. Now you can ask, what if we could have even more-efficient nouns? You are introducing Verbs-Nouns dimensions of reality, in terms that a Nouns-only reality can begin to perceive. Focusing only on your leading-edge understanding of the cool features of learning and developing sounds to them like you are not grounded. Stay grounded and add the benefits of some verbs.

This logic works all the way up through the ESH levels. Start with what they can see as real in your world. Then you can begin to see if they might see the value of beginning to add dimensions of the next level.

What do you do if you are communicating with someone whose reality includes higher dimensions than yours? You might be working with a Verbs-Nouns (VN) reality, while they appear to be working from an LVN or ESH level. You might perceive that they can see things you can't. You can invite them to share what they see. It is most helpful if you clarify with them that it is most useful to you if they can explain it first in terms you can understand–in verbs and nouns. Then they can begin to show you the value of adding dimensions from LVN or ESH. The point is to communicate with others. If you experience that you want to communicate with someone else and that it seems like you are talking about completely different things, while still in relatively the same context, maybe you are assuming different levels of perceived reality. Ask. See if you can get to a shared understanding at the Nouns-only level. Then you can try the Verbs-Nouns level, and so on.

The good news is that we all have all of these levels of perceived reality within us, so we can access all four of these levels of perceived reality. And the agreements we tend to work with in some groups exclude some of them, making communication difficult. Since you already have the dimensions within you, you can still access them and ask the question. It is your choice.

WHERE PEOPLE ARE SAYING YES! IN THEIR OWN WAY

The initial conditions you start with, your Yes! or your No!, impact what your agreements field looks like for you. And you can shift them, for yourself and for your group. The cost of not saying Yes! What is the cost of No!, the costs of scarcity? The cost of entropy. Where are people saying Yes!?

A sampling of what is possible out there. Of what my colleagues and I are discovering. This exploration started consciously in 2004, as my colleagues and I were being invited to visit with groups that were considered extraordinary in their behaviors. My group at the ISC was known for being creative in thinking strategically and systemically about complex organizations. Early examples included a community health center in South Texas, a training institute for dentists in Nevada, a toy store in Moscow, a textile mill in North Carolina. We were being asked to study these groups to understand what it was they were doing. The people inviting us had tried and could not quite figure it out. They had identified these very high-performing groups, but these groups had not been able to tell them what differentiated them.

Soon after these initial explorations, we started an initiative that we call the Global Pactoecographic Collaborative. Global because we are finding these very-high-performing groups everywhere around the globe. Pactoecography is the study of agreements fields mapping. Collaborative because we are coming together. This is a network of people, working together, collaborating, and generating these understandings. These understandings are building our understanding of the human agreenome. A global exploration initiative, with the goal of describing the geometric structure of the agreements field, which we have been exploring in the previous chapters. We are identifying and mapping the full continuum of human agreements, what they are, what causes them, and what the consequences are. We are trying to sequence map all of the agreements together, known as the agreements of the members of our species, *Homo lumens*.

What are we finding? We have examples that we can share briefly from Africa, Latin America, the US, and Europe? The point is that it is happening in many different places around the world.

Through the free, online Agreements Health Check survey, the Global Pactoecographic Collaborative (GPC) has identified examples of people saying Yes!, in their own way, in 126 countries. We currently have over 196,000 responses. We can start with South Africa and colleagues of ours at Meshfield and the University of Cape Town. They have been working on two fascinating projects, which you can read about online at isclarity.org, bringing complementary currencies to townships in South Africa, developing regenerative water and regenerative building projects. Learning what they are learning, across thousands to hundreds of thousands of people within these complex social systems of the townships. How did they discover what they are learning? They shared that with each other, through youth ambassadors. Finding ways to support them with their own funding, through complementary currencies which were amazingly supported by local NGOs, local government, local academia, and local companies, all coming together as a big network. Even supported by local and national government, and international foundations. What have they learned about how people come together, to see their future, saying Yes! to it? The group in South Africa is now working on ways to bring sustainable energy within communities that are often excluded through the first brownouts within the city. They have found ways to fund the development of their own energy, for themselves, by themselves, with themselves. They do the same for local agriculture and local water systems. How do we come together to say Yes! to our future around us? Meshfield is leading the way in these communities, learning how to say Yes! together, even within a system that is working against them.

In Costa Rica, we are working with the University of International Cooperation, which has existed now for decades, bringing a sustainable way of looking at agriculture and community development across Costa Rica. Now working as Regenerate Costa Rica, bringing together experts from different parts of the system, from the political, agricultural, economic, cultural, and social, saying Yes! to regenerative community at the scale of all of Costa Rica. As an example, for the world, of how people can work, from the very local to the national. Local action to national policy.

As an example of what is possible in Mexico, working with a large multinational microfinance bank, demonstrating that it is possible to satisfy multiple stakeholders. Supporting the very poor in becoming productive entrepreneurs, generating their own capacity to regenerate their own future, at scale, while supporting that initiative through access to the global marketplace of capital. How does one do both the work of the NGO, of serving at a very local level, and the level of scaling that is something governments typically do, and doing that with business? Doing that in a profitable way that generates its own revenues, its own source of capital. This bank is figuring out how to do that, regeneratively, at scale.

In the USA, a community health center, Gateway, has consistently outperformed other community health centers, through many grant cycles, in delivering far greater health to their local community than even seen in most major hospitals and healthcare systems. So how is this community health center in an economically poor community able to thrive and offer such amazing services? How are they able to bring the community together and collaborate, saying Yes! at a much higher level?

In the book *Ecosynomics*, I describe work that we did from the mid-2000s with a textile mill in North Carolina. Building on work of the previous thirty years by its founder, bringing the community together, through their Yes! in service to their customers. They provided products that increased not just the comfort of their feet but also increased preventive foot health, while offering a product that provides for the families of the people working at the company.

A group called YOUnify, bringing together people from across multiple spectrums to say there is a Yes! that everyone can agree to. Looking at who they are within this country, from the very local level of neighborhoods to the national level. People can cross political divides, ideological divides, sectorial divides, and say this is theirs to do. How do they come together to say Yes! to something, as a community, where there are great divisions across ideologies, across the political spectrum and across sectors? They can come together, and they can demonstrate the impact and value of coming together.

There are now many examples of initiatives that ISC and its network have done across Europe. Bringing together the building sector, to say that they can retrofit all of the building stock, over the next 30 years, within Europe to greatly reduce greenhouse gas emissions. One example of this is the Renovate Europe campaign, supporting the European commission and parliament in getting to a solution that all new buildings in Europe must be nearly net zero as of 2018. How does one get so many countries and some of the leaders, that are divided in so many ways, to come together to say Yes! to something so audacious? Which will cost trillions of euros to do. They bring everybody together to say Yes! to this future, together. To the impact it will have on their health, their economics, their environment, all at the same time. These are all initiatives affiliated with the Global Pactoecographic Collaborative through the Human Agreenome project.

Other examples of groups that are taking on their own agreements, are Harvard's Center for Health and the Global Environment which, until recently under the leadership of Jack Spengler, is looking at environmental health—the impact on air, water, buildings—and how people can come together to understand what is possible in environmental health, training the next generation of leaders, and providing the basic research that shows what clean air, water, and buildings can do to our health. The Center for Work, Health and Well-being at the Harvard T.H. Chan School of Public Health is looking at thriving from work. How can one be better because of the way one works? What is the impact of that work on the way people do that work? Of thriving on the characteristics of the enterprise? Does the health of your agreements field have a direct impact on the efficiency of your interventions, your activities, the outputs from the different functional areas of your organization, what each area contributes to, the impact they have for others within your ecosystem? The Human Flourishing Program at Harvard is measuring flourishing, community well-being, meaning and purpose, trying to understand and come to consensus on ways of measuring and demonstrating the value of human flourishing. What it is and what it leads to, with very simple measures that we can all agree upon and test, at scale. The Oxford Character Project, is showing how character and virtues are a critical part of what it means to say Yes! to humanity. What that means for people as leaders. What do character and virtue do? What can the humanities teach about what character education for leaders does? How leaders develop character and how that impacts their communities and the outcomes they can achieve.

Within ITESM's EGADE business school, courses on strategy and sustainability are demonstrating, with leadership from the Dean, what it means to say Yes!, across the business school, within a larger system. That organizations across Mexico can say Yes! to treating people as a valuable resource, that they are learning ways to thrive in organizations, ways to bring out the best in everyone, in their own terms. Of saying Yes! to human agreements, bringing healthier human agreements as a normal practice being taught within the business school.

In Madrid at the Technical University of Madrid (UPM), where I was on the advisory board of the Technology Innovation Center for Human Development, bringing a human-centered way of looking at technological development. You can achieve far better results, far greater impact, for the environment, for humanity, right now. Supported by large industry, the academy, the city, government at different levels, from the European to the Spanish to the city of Madrid. They are coming together to learn how to collaborate deeply, across disciplines, to bring about human development through technology, with technology. At UPM's Center for Leadership and Technology, bringing innovative ways to leadership thinking. It is possible to say Yes! to abundance, to say Yes! to human creativity. These are very practical ways, within the technological university that you can do that, for your leadership, every day.

Another great example is the certificate for Chief Happiness Officers, offered by the WOHASU Foundation and Florida International University, developing the skill sets needed to be able to say Yes! to human creativity, within each person, within their teams and organizations.

These examples, across all of these countries, within the Human Agreenome, show that there is great scarcity in disengagement. Across the globe, lots of people are living at the very high end, experiencing very strong agreements fields, with very healthy human agreements fields. They are experimenting with this. We can learn with them, and from them. ISC's Agreements Health Check survey shows that maybe these groups are everywhere, all around the world. We have found them in 126 countries. Instead of looking only to a few global centers of financial wealth, to those who have a lot of money, and who do not have strong agreements fields, maybe you can start looking around you, locally where you are. Those who know how to do what they are doing. As you take steps toward greater vibrancy, you have local examples of what healthier agreements look like. You can start to have your own Yes!, with your own local examples of how people have figured out how to do this, within your own local context. How to say Yes!, within your culture, in your moment, to human creativity, your Yes!

CHAPTER 9

YOUR INVITATION TO ENGAGE

I started with your initial conditions. Living with a Yes! or a No! You saw that you have a preference. You know what your Yes! is. What it looks like. You saw what an agreements field is. What the choices are that you have, the choices you are making. How you can measure that, with your own scorecard, for yourself. Your Big Yes! Your Impact Resilience Scorecard. For the Yes! for your community, your organization, your team. What the costs of not doing it are. What people around the globe are starting to do already.

I invite you to engage. You can do this, on many different levels, in many different ways. On your own. Take what you have seen, in all the different exercises that I have invited you to do. All these boxes of exercises, the group questions I provided. Do this on your own. Go try it and see if it works. That would be fantastic because you are doing something for your Yes! Saying Yes! to your agreements.

I also invite you to share with others. Pay forward what you have learned. Just like the examples I provided did. Let others know what you are learning about what works, at whatever level you are at. Any movement is a huge gift to humanity. A move from very deep scarcity is very difficult. Improving difficult agreements fields makes them better, even if only slightly better. How do we move from okay to much better? How do we develop ecologies of sacred hospitality, within our local communities? Having massive impacts, with very little effort, at any level. Sharing with others is also a gift that I will receive and that you will receive from others.

Share with us through the Institute for Strategic Clarity, the Global Pactoecographic Collaborative, the Human Agreenome Project, the different institutions within our network. Share with us. Share what you are learning. Share what your questions are. Share where you are in your process. Share what you are sharing with your community. Your writings, videos, audios, conferences, gatherings, meetings. Share with us how you are sharing, and what you are learning.

You can also work directly with us. Be part of the Global Pactoecographic Collaborative. Be part of the Human Agreenome Project. Contribute directly. Contact me. We can discover how you can make a direct contribution. What your unique gift is, what you want to bring. The data you have. The questions you are asking. The places where you can go and try something. Where others from around the Global Pactoecographic Collaborative network can come together and serve that beingness with you.

The key thing I want you to take away in this invitation to engage is a choice. It is your choice. In this time together, we have shown that your choices make a difference. Your choices start with either a Yes! or a No! This is what that choice looks like, what the agreements field looks like. These are the choices that you are saying Yes! or No! to. These are the benefits and the costs of them. These are the ways you can measure them. These are the ways that you can adjust, when you see what you really want to say Yes! to. What you know is yours to do. Your Yes! It is your choice.

Another way to engage is through reading clubs. You can find questions to start a reading club at isclarity.org. You can look at ISC's onboarding platform for documents describing the systemic approaches, like the GRASP framework we explored earlier in the book. You can dive into mapping your operating system, and learn how to understand it through systems mapping with strategic clarity. You can learn more about the agreements field and the different dimensions in your choices with the SCAN onboarding document. You can access these documents for free on ISC's onboarding platform. Like reading groups that have formed in Europe, the USA, Mexico, and Guatemala, you can explore our blog posts, which are short readings about specific ideas related to your agreements field. Sometimes they are about other groups, what other authors are discovering. Through these readings, your reading club can connect into the network of what is happening within the Human Agreenome Project, the Global Pactoecographic Collaborative, other reading clubs. You can explore our books *Managing from Clarity*, *Ecosynomics*. At isclarity.org we provide questions that you can work with, at each level, from where you are. You can bring a group together. We provide different forms for ways to work with the group, doing it online, doing it in person, doing a mix. There are different ways you can work with groups of people you are finding. If you find new ways, share those with us also.

You can also engage with us to research what you are asking. Whether you are on your own, in an organization, a researcher at an independent institute or in academia. What different questions interest you? What emerging questions are you seeing? What do you think are interesting areas to explore in the agreements field, in the strength of the agreements field? What is the impact of that? What are local applications that you are seeing? Where we can engage? You can connect to a global network of people working within the Global Pactoecographic Collaborative. If you are a consultant, you can take it into organizational processes. You can work with coaches who can work with you individually or as a team, developing your capacities.

You can try this on your own, teaching. I am a teacher. Many of the people within our community are teachers. They teach in universities, high schools, grade schools, executive education. You can teach groups of friends, or within your own organization. Teaching within different reference disciplines. As a sociologist, an economist, a political scientist, a cultural anthropologist, an engineer. Bring different reference disciplines to this, maturing with us. What you are learning, how you are seeing it, connecting with others, within your reference discipline as well as the applied disciplines. Within medicine, education, business. Within different areas within these applied disciplines, such as epidemiology, oncology, pediatrics. Within marketing, finance, strategy, operations, and accounting within the business school. What are the different disciplines? What are different levels? Connecting with others, through the Global Pactoecographic Collaborative who are teaching it within your domain, at your level, sharing with others what you are learning. Showing where this applies, to what contexts. The point is that you are invited to engage, for yourself or with others, in your local community or with us.

We want to learn what you are learning because that is the Human Agreenome Project. What are we learning as humanity, in each and every instance? What does the topography of human agreements look like? The Human Agreenome Project within the Global Pactoecographic Collaborative.

You are welcome, and we look forward to meeting you, to engaging with you, to engaging your Yes! Your future depends on it. Our future depends on it. It is a choice. It is your choice. It is your Yes!